Bible Interpretations

Tenth Series
October 1 - December 24, 1893

*Romans, I & II Corinthians, Ephesians,
Colossians, James, I Peter, Revelation*

Bible Interpretations

Tenth Series

Romans, I & II Corinthians, Ephesians, Colossians, James, I Peter, Revelation

These Bible Interpretations were published in the Inter-Ocean Newspaper in Chicago, Illinois during the late eighteen nineties.

By
Emma Curtis Hopkins

President of the Emma Curtis Hopkins Theological Seminary in Chicago, Illinois

WISEWOMAN PRESS

Bible Interpretations: Tenth Series

By Emma Curtis Hopkins

© WiseWoman Press 2011

Managing Editor: Michael Terranova

ISBN: 978-0945385-60-8

WiseWoman Press

Vancouver, WA 98665

www.wisewomanpress.com

www.emmacurtishopkins.com

CONTENTS

      Foreword by Rev. Natalie R. Jean vi
      Introduction by Rev. Michael Terranova viii

I.   When the Truth is Known 1
      Romans 1: 1-19

II.   Justification; free grace, redemption 10
      Romans 3:19-26

III. Justification by Faith 19
      Romans 5:1-11

IV. Christian Living 27
      Romans 12:1-15

V.   Comments and Explanations on The Golden Text ... 37
      I Corinthians 8: 1-13

VI. Science of the Christ Principle 44
      I Corinthians 12:1-26

VII. The Grace of Liberality 51
      II Corinthians 8:1-12

VIII. Imitation of Christ 59
      Ephesians 4:20-32

IX. The Christian Home 67
      Colossians 3:12-25

X.   Grateful Obedience 74
      James 1:16-27

XI. The Heavenly Inheritance 81
      I Peter 1:1-12

XII. The Glorified Saviour 87
      Revelation 1:9-20

XIII. A Christmas Lesson 93
      Matthew 2:1-11

XIV. REVIEW 101
      List of Bible Interpretation Series 113

Editors Note

All lessons starting with the Seventh Series of Bible Interpretations will be Sunday postings from the Inter-Ocean Newspaper in Chicago, Illinois. Many of the lessons in the following series were retrieved from the International New Thought Association Archives, in Mesa, Arizona by, Rev Joanna Rogers. Many others were retrieved from libraries in Chicago, and the Library of Congress, by Rev. Natalie Jean.

All the lessons follow the Sunday School Lesson Plan published in "Peloubet's International Sunday School Lessons". The passages to be studied are selected by an International Committee of traditional Bible Scholars.

Some of the Emma's lessons don't have a title. In these cases the heading will say "Comments and Explanations of the Golden Text," followed by the Bible passages to be studied.

Foreword

By Rev. Natalie R. Jean

I have read many teachings by Emma Curtis Hopkins, but the teachings that touch the very essence of my soul are her Bible Interpretations. There are many books written on the teachings of the Bible, but none can touch the surface of the true messages more than these Bible interpretations. With each word you can feel and see how Spirit spoke through Emma. The mystical interpretations take you on a wonderful journey to Self Realization.

Each passage opens your consciousness to a new awareness of the realities of life. The illusions of life seem to disappear through each interpretation. Emma teaches that we are the key that unlocks the doorway to the light that shines within. She incorporates ideals of other religions into her teachings, in order to understand the commonalities, so that there is a complete understanding of our Oneness. Emma opens our eyes and mind to a better today and exciting future.

Emma Curtis Hopkins, one of the Founders of New Thought teaches us to love ourselves, to speak our Truth, and to focus on our Good. My life has moved in wonderful directions because of her teachings. I know the only thing that can move me in this world is God. May these interpretations guide you to a similar path and may you truly remember that "There Is Good For You and You Ought to Have It."

Introduction

Emma Curtis Hopkins was born in 1849 in Killingsly, Connecticut. She passed on April 8, 1925. Mrs. Hopkins had a marvelous education and could read many of the worlds classical texts in their original language. During her extensive studies she was always able to discover the Universal Truths in each of the world's sacred traditions. She quotes from many of these teachings in her writings. As she was a very private person, we know little about her personal life. What we do know has been gleaned from other people or from the archived writings we have been able to discover.

Emma Curtis Hopkins was one of the greatest influences on the New Thought movement in the United States. She taught over 50,000 people the Universal Truth of knowing "God is All there is." She taught many of founders of early New Thought, and in turn these individuals expanded the influence of her teachings. All of her writings encourage the student to enter into a personal relationship with God. She presses us to deny anything except the Truth of this spiritual Presence in every area of our lives. This is the central focus of all her teachings.

The first six series of Bible Interpretations were presented at her seminary in Chicago, Illinois. The remaining Series', probably close to thirty, were printed in the Inter Ocean Newspaper in Chicago. Many of the lessons are no longer available for various reasons. It is the intention of WiseWoman Press to publish as many of these Bible Interpretations as possible. Our hope is that any missing lessons will be found or directed to us.

I am very honored to join the long line of people that have been involved in publishing Emma Curtis Hopkins's Bible Interpretations. Some confusion exists as to the numbering sequence of the lessons. In the early 1920's many of the lessons were published by the Highwatch Fellowship. Inadvertently the first two lessons were omitted from the numbering system. Rev. Joanna Rogers has corrected this mistake by finding the first two lessons and restoring them to their rightful place in the order. Rev. Rogers has been able to find many of the missing lessons at the International New Thought Alliance archives in Mesa, Arizona. Rev. Rogers painstakingly scoured the archives for the missing lessons as well as for Mrs. Hopkins other works. She has published much of what was discovered. WiseWoman Press is now publishing the correctly numbered series of the Bible Interpretations.

In the early 1940's, there was a resurgence of interest in Emma's works. At that time, Highwatch Fellowship began to publish many of her writings, and it was then that *High Mysticism*, her seminal work was published. Previously, the material contained in High Mysticism was only available as individual lessons and was brought together in book form for the first time. Although there were many errors in these first publications and many Bible verses were incorrectly quoted, I am happy to announce that WiseWoman Press is now publishing *High Mysticism* in the a corrected format. This corrected form was scanned faithfully from the original, individual lessons.

The next person to publish some of the Bible Lessons was Rev. Marge Flotron from the Ministry of Truth International in Chicago, Illinois. She published the Bible Lessons as well as many of Emma's other works. By her initiative, Emma's writings were brought to a larger audience when DeVorss & Company, a longtime publisher of Truth Teachings, took on the publication of her key works.

In addition, Dr. Carmelita Trowbridge, founding minister of The Sanctuary of Truth in Alhambra, California, inspired her assistant minister, Rev. Shirley Lawrence, to publish many of Emma's works, including the first three series of Bible Interpretations. Rev. Lawrence created mail order courses for many of these Series. She has graciously passed on any information she had, in order to assure that these works continue to inspire individuals and groups who are called to further study of the teachings of Mrs. Hopkins.

Finally, a very special acknowledgement goes to Rev Natalie Jean, who has worked diligently to retrieve several of Emma's lessons from the Library of Congress, as well as libraries in Chicago. Rev. Jean hand-typed many of the lessons she found on microfilm. Much of what she found is on her website, www.highwatch.net.

It is with a grateful heart that I am able to pass on these wonderful teachings. I have been studying dear Emma's works for fifteen years. I was introduced to her writings by my mentor and teacher, Rev. Marcia Sutton. I have been overjoyed with the results of delving deeply into these Truth Teachings.

In 2004, I wrote a Sacred Covenant entitled "Resurrecting Emma," and created a website, www.emmacurtishopkins.com. The result of creating this covenant and website has brought many of Emma's works into my hands and has deepened my faith in God. As a result of my love for these works, I was led to become a member of Wise-Woman Press and to publish these wonderful teachings. God is Good.

My understanding of Truth from these divinely inspired teachings keeps bringing great Joy, Freedom, and Peace to my life.

Dear reader; It is with an open heart that I offer these works to you, and I know they will touch you as they have touched me. Together we are living in the Truth that God is truly present, and living for and through each of us.

The greatest Truth Emma presented to us is "My Good is my God, Omnipresent, Omnipotent and Omniscient."

Rev. Michael Terranova
WiseWoman Press
Vancouver, Washington, 2010

LESSON I

When the Truth is Known

Romans 1: 1-19

The Idea of a Saviour to come was held by the ancient Romans. In the time of Octavius Caesar Tacitus and Seutonius, both tell of the sacred books of the priests, which declare that the men of Judea shall subjugate the nations and all things to their dominion.

A Judean finally appeared whose teachings contained within their quality the elements of mastery over every other teaching. It was of this man's principles that Paul, the Jewish lawyer, wrote, *"I am not ashamed of the gospel of Christ, for it is the power of God unto salvation to every one that believeth.* (Rom. 1:16)." The gospel of Christ was peculiar in that it took some of the current and favored teachings of philosophy and religion and united them into one scientific explanation of how the universe is run end what is its destiny.

He had taken Plato's proposition that "God is truth," and demonstrated that truth is a healing prospering substance, he was a practical illustration of the saying, which was preserved from the pen of some thoughtful sage of an almost unknown past, found, on a tablet in the valley of Hebron after the flood: "Truth is not troubled by matter nor cumbered by body; but is naked, clean, unchangeable. Truth is only in eternal bodies, which very bodies are truth." He told men that before Abraham was he had been, and that he in himself was changeless substance.

He took the conclusion of philosophers, after their ages of profound study, as the basic principle of his science of life. "Ideas are the only real things." God is the ruling principle.

When the Truth Is Known

He taught the science of faith, showing how the vitality and health of man might be renewed through countless generations by the perpetual renewal of faith. But he showed that no man could possibly have faith very long unless he knew truth. His whole teaching was to show that every expectation, hope, and wish of man are fulfilable through knowing truth, sin, disease, and disappointment must cease when the truth is known.

Faith is the confidence of mind in something good. At first mankind might have to believe in the wisdom and kindness of a God they could not see, but afterward they would believe because they had seen. He illustrated this by sending forth his disciples without changes of raiment, shoes, or money, and letting them see that they could be provided for by their faith in the watch care of an unseen deity. Having proved that, he next sent them out with everything customary for travelers in those times to show them that no matter what are the usages of mankind suitable provisions will always accompany them. The new customs of later ages would bring new exhibitions of watch care. When Edward, the Black Prince, was hard besieged at the battle of Cressy, he sent in hot haste for his Father, who was watching the battle, to forward him re-enforcements. His father replied: "Tell Edward I am not so inexperienced a soldier as not to know when to send re-enforcements, and not so careless a father as not to send them when I see they are necessary,"

Faith in God

Thus the divine watch care never absent from man, is not scornful of re-enforcing the empty meal barrel of the widow, nor the depleted purse of the father of a family. He who believes this is more alive in his body and stronger in his intellect than he who does not believe it if we judge by observation. In the tenth verse of this chapter Paul tells of having faith that he would have a prosperous journey because, like Edward the Black Prince, he had prayed, and like Edward he was willing to believe he could get on without a prosperous journey if his father saw best not to send it. This simple confidence had a very energizing effect upon Paul. It was just the very state of mind the Christ Jesus had taught was the subjugating quality. As the science of mind, he had shown that mind may read the book of its own life history and prophecy in all that it senses. As the science of faith he had shown that pure discernment or the discernment of purity is Jesus Christ or the action of truth in man.

*Whatever of fear, hope or joy we sense, we ought to know that it tells the history of our past thoughts and prophesies how our mind is running into the future. A thoughtful woman had seen enough of astral phenomena to convince her that there are imps of the air. Her informers had not explained that those powers of darkness they showed were exhibitions of their belief in evil principles; if they had she would not have believed in their power. After a while she saw some dark objects on her own account while nobody was present. She was reading her own meditations in legible text. She had the ability to discern how they were her projected, thought substance covered with veils of false information. The discernment itself would have come out clearly if she had said promptly, "I do not believe in any information of evil I have ever received. I believe in goodness only." The false would have fallen off and she could have seen how strong her thought quality was. After that she could have had prosperity instead of defeat and failure.

She made imp quality her father or faith, and of course that kind of a father sent re-enforcements of imps. Paul sent up his faith to a divine throne of supply.

Discerning The Good

There is the pure discerning power in us all whereby we can see the good and pure in all things unveiled. It is the quick sight of undressed gold in all things, we are told that to hear of the purity of each man, woman and child is so pleasant a doctrine that at first we are glad to get it, but upon putting it into practice we rebel. (Rev. 10:10) Unchaste, untruthful people exhibit veils we have been covering our faith substance with exactly as the imp exhibited hers.

We have a discerning eye for the gold in all things and stamp that gold with what we please, as Jesus discerned the gold in the fish and stamped it with legal formulas. There is a gold basis among men to symbolize the good base of all things. The instant you are a discerner of good, gold will be plentiful with you. This is the truth concerning gold finding. <u>The symbol follows the principle</u>. *"Therein is the righteousness of God revealed."* (Rom. 1:17). "<u>From faith to faith</u>." That is, <u>from faith in both good and evil to faith in good only</u>.

"The Just shall live by faith." The discerning faculty is a life-energizing faculty. <u>You will always notice that a just mind discerns good in a situation</u>. Then the very faculty itself is self-supporting.

It does not need either good or evil to live on; it lives on itself.

"The true light now shineth," is Jesus Christ still present in the world. It is the illuminating moment of mind that comes suddenly while it is reasoning on the divine side. The true mind is not a believer that if a man knows all there is of music he takes away from his neighbor's privilege to know all there is of music. Such a belief is lighted by the two earth candlesticks of Revelation. "Music is good. The lack of it is bad." These are the two ideas on music which now light the world. The true light on that theme is that all mankind have the whole harmony of God open to their free use.

So of health, so of intelligence. This is a statement wholly independent of the candles. It is a sunshine all by itself. It is Jesus Christ. Whoever believes it is illuminated in mind and sees that the truth of it is his confidence. He finds that he himself is the true light that now shineth.

The Faithful Man is Strong

The self-feeding nature of faith is its glory. It causes a man to pay no heed to stories of evil and no heed to stories of good. He knows what he knows and nobody hides his knowledge by words. You can see for yourself that this is a masterful doctrine, Jesus of Nazareth, born in Judea, brought it out by speech and practice. It takes the teaching of ought and ought not and makes raga of it at once.

It shows that in so far as man has ignored the oughts and ought nots of other men he has been free. "You ought to be a poor man of a low caste and ought not to try to illumine your age," was the opinion of men on Euripides, but he ignored it and it was written of him that "the glory of the Athenian stage descended into the tomb with him."

"You ought to throw your baby into the Ganges," is said to the eastern mother. "You ought not to throw your baby into the river," says the western candlestick. But child mortality is equally prevalent under both instructions. "You ought to be beautiful," is said to women, and they paint and grimace and curl and pinch till they are the ugliest creatures in creation. "You ought not to be beautiful," is said to men, till they are the worst acting things on the planet. There is no ought not to Jesus Christ. He shines by his own knowledge of truth. By the true light there are no plenty and poverty of the divine gifts. The gifts are man's own self-supplying faith.

"The mental motive cannot be hidden." Luther, Lincoln, Jesus, were surrounded seemingly by powerful traitors, but their motives are all now exposed. John says that the spirit of God in such men caused them to stand upright and ascend into heaven in the sight of their enemies. The pure motive of Jesus Christ triumphant while yet you are alive. The pure motive in mind makes mind and life entirely consistent. Under the confident belief that man is a sinner the man of pure motive, to be consistent with his faith, sees that he must go to the extremity of his doctrine, and like Paul, must call himself "chief of sinners." *Love it!*

Glory of a Pure Motive

The man of pure or single motives always stands out as a great character among his companions. He believes in himself, and one who believes in himself is always great. He goes to extremes in his principles. If he sees that he is chief of sinners he must see that he is Satan. If he sees that he is good he must see that the extreme is that he is God. At this height of proclamation he sees that he is neither God nor Satan, but something incomparably greater and immeasurably different from any word. He sees that he is his own pure motive. He lives on this substance. It is his defense and strength and glory in its outward showing. It puts the moon under his feet and the sun around him for his reputation, but he like the woman in Revelation, is something remarkably different from his reputation. His knowledge of this is Jesus Christ, the power of God with salvation. The power of Jesus Christ was the Holy Ghost substance. It is everywhere present. Seeing all these outcomes of the gospel, it is no wonder Paul was "not ashamed of it". This faith is the sight, hearing, touch, of the Holy Ghost substance which is to confront the world. It is the light of any mind that it, and out of it whatever we choose to make we can make.

John said that nine-tenths of the inhabitants of the world would look up and rejoice when such a stupendous truth should shine out <u>as that God is the ruling principle</u>, that God is mind, <u>but that the ruling principle is something as usable by pure motive as flour and wool, and that he who uses the ruling principle is not really nameable, though named as purpose of God, is undescribable, free, and untouchable as purity Itself, though purity is his garment.</u> One tenth will consider it sacrilege, and that consideration will destroy them. The service of Paul with his "sprit in this gospel" being consistent now makes itself manifest. This is the Holy Ghost which Jesus Christ used to make all things.

Inter-Ocean Newspaper, October 1, 1893

LESSON II

Justification; free grace, redemption

Romans 3:19-26

Justification; free grace, redemption, according to the most scientific and spiritual sense of this New Testament, is the theme of to-day's Bible lesson, Rom. 3:19-26.

We will take free grace first because the golden text reads, *"Being justified freely by his grace,"* as if we could not be justified in conduct, speech, thought, faith till we had received of free grace.

The most auspicious example of free grace on record is that of the malefactor on the cross. The simplest and commonest is the experience of every practitioner of metaphysical healing. The metaphysical reasoners who understand how to think so as to fill the mental atmosphere around a sick man with healing have often noticed that they may be conscious of the man's having only one disease about him and may actually be only trying to cure one disease, but will cure three or four other accompanying diseases by simply trying to cure one. <u>This is free grac</u>e. The three or four unsound spots have been oiled out of existence by the unction visited upon the principal one. There was a total unsoundness in the malefactor's case. He had committed every sort of iniquity he could get a chance at, and had had a mind to commit a great deal more. He faced his whole quality up and was utterly disgusted at himself when he saw the facts of the case. He acknowledged himself worthy of the utmost punishment, but realizing the great power and kindness of Jesus he asked humbly if such a great blessing might be vouchsafed him as the memory of him by the good man near him, "Lord, remember me when thou comest into the thy kingdom."

Free Grace.

The cure was instantaneous. The mental state, the conduct, the records of the past, were blotted out, and he was taken suddenly into utter forgiveness. *"This day shalt thou be with me in Paradise."* <u>That was free grace</u>. <u>Nothing more was ever to come of his past. His present had nothing promissory of evil.</u> Clean, glad, equal with Jesus in Paradise.

Every one of us has partaken somewhat of free grace. We were perhaps, afraid that some accident would befall us, but in our morning prayer we had put ourselves into the something bordering on the attitude of the malefactor on the cross, and the unction thereof anointed or oiled our way safely through what was intended to be accident. More close resemblance to the malefactor's attitude of mind is free grace through more difficult passages. Bunyan looked out and saw a ragged, swearing, intoxicated man reeling along. "But for the grace of God there goes John Bunyan," he said. During one of his prayers, or during some one's preaching, or while some one was singing, he had received free grace enough to take away his appetite and also his slum tendencies of conduct.

James the brother of Jesus said that there was nothing would hide or oil away the consequences of so many sins as getting the doctrine on that pull of it which changed a man's or woman's conduct so that he no longer cared to act the former way. "He that converteth one from the error of his ways hideth a multitude of sins." Some people see that it is not according to Christian doctrine or according to the results of Christian doctrine to use other men's money in their business unknown to the men. It is a hard pull for them, but they stop detaining funds unlawfully. If their heart is not in the right action it is like the well-ordered conduct of State's prisoners. Their conduct cometh not of free grace, which oils up outer actions, making them easy. If these converts preach of Christian science they will be sure to lay great stress on living the life; acting outwardly.

On the Gloomy Side

They give themselves away. It is clear that there is something hard for them to give up. Some people see that it is not according to Christian doctrine, nor to the results thereof to look upon the gloomy side of life. They must not think of the dark and dismal points of their career. They have had ideas which brought them out into hard place, and they see that it is by the pathway of a new set of ideas they must get into green pastures and still waters. So they speak and think deliberately and willfully on the Christian science side. Their talk will be all about speaking and thinking cheerfully, speaking and thinking scientifically. They give themselves away that it is very hard, indeed, for them to hold their thoughts steady to spiritual transcendency. They would like to mourn and whine. They dare not stop repeating high themes lest their hearts breaks. It is no effort for them to behave themselves outwardly. They have no outer temptation. They do not get angry and swear, use money dishonestly, make themselves free with other people's spouses, nor hold consultations to put down their neighbors doctrines. They have only inward temptations to see the world in the pessimistic order. They have always great power in word and thought. They bring to pass by the gathering energy of persistence.

They have not received of free grace enough so that they realize the ease and comfort of right thoughts. They do not lie down in the safety of feeling that they cannot think dangerously.

Free grace justifies thoughts so that no evil can result from them even though they were not according to authority. Free grace justifies conduct so that nothing evil can result there-from though never so silly.

~~XXX~~ <u>He who has tasted of free grace is so happy that he never thinks whether anything is right or wrong.</u> He is redeemed from right and wrong. *"Justified freely by his grace, which is redemption in Christ Jesus."* <u>He is always sure it is just the way the spirit meant it to be no matter what happened</u>. He has received the unction from on high. He eats of hidden manna. He has a name or feeling which none can understand save whosoever hath received likewise.

"Now the righteousness of God without the law is manifested."

Daniel and Elisha

Some people have seen how safely Daniel met the lions and Elisha met the army, when they had said just as foolish things and behaved just as weakly as other Jews, and have been bound to get scot free from their past thoughts and conduct on the proclamation of entire freedom from law. Everything about the lawless Jesus, the lawless Elisha, the lawless mystics, enchants them and enchants the hearers. Their very vehemence gives them away as flowing satisfaction. High themes to them are easy as breathing. They have received free grace thereon. Transcendent uprightness is easy to them as beauty and youth for only the young and beautiful ever accept the doctrine of the lawless Jesus, and it is sure restoration of youth and beauty to accept it. But still they show that they are carefully fingering some finer springs of the golden door of "the adoption to wit, the redemption in Christ Jesus."

It may be one spring, and it may be another for them, for us, for you, which accepting free grace, justifies us in all things we do and say and feel, so that every instant we work some miracle, purposely or unpurposely, but this is certain, "the adoption to wit, the redemption in Christ Jesus," is the unction within the name, Jesus Christ.

Power from Obedience

It was by obedience to the name he used that Jesus Christ had the keys of the universe committed to his charge. He did not have the supreme unction from purely Devoid Being till in one supreme moment of utter ignorance, utter humiliation, he struck the last spring of the golden door. This was the lowest and the highest spring all in one. Having disrobed himself of knowledge, disrobed himself of power, in this estate he recognized a will inscrutable, which besides being mine is thine and he cried, *"Thy will be done."*

Noting that instant was not in that sense he himself meant to be, though he had wrought miracles of many mighty kinds. Now hath his name become the door to the name. Within it is the hidden manna. Within it is free grace. Within it is justification of everything we say, or think or do. Within it is miracle working. Within it is the manifestation of Jesus Christ as he is now after having ascended into heaven, sat on the right hand of power and drawn such as he pleased to proclaim his visible presence among men where they choose to be himself; his invisible presence where they choose to speak of him in the third person.

The crowning sublimity of the divinity within all men, equally fixed, is its obedience. "Depart out of our coasts!" screamed the whole city of the Gadarenes, to Jesus Christ when he was the visibility of divinity. And he obeyed them like a willing child. He had shown that his influence would change their whole conduct, change their whole mind, change their whole disposition.

Fidelity to His Name

We have wondered why his conduct of life has never been observed by the Christian church simply because they ordered his name out on the coast of business methods. We have wondered why Christian scientists who have the most spiritual doctrine of all that is now preached, do not have the mind that was in Christ Jesus. They have ordered him out of their coast. They have said that we should have all the afflictions and hardships of Jesus Christ if we repeated his name. They have said it was a superstition to repeat it constantly. This was ordering it out of their mental coasts. Those who dwell on the coasts where behavior is their god will buy and sell, converse and manage with security of prosperity and favor if they call upon the divine nature to arrive again as Jesus Christ into their life coasts of daily transactions.

The beauty and sublimity of Jesus Christ is in his obedience. "Depart out of our coasts!" He goes, "Arrive on our coasts!" He arrives. Those who have made the right state of mind their god will think and speak with security of pleasure if they call upon the divine nature to arrive again as Jesus Christ in their mind, even to the miracle working thereof. "Arrive on that coast." He arrives.

He Is God

Those who have made the lawlessness of Jesus Christ, their god, and have walked over the earth as kings and princes thereof, will touch the last spring of the golden door of God in the name, Jesus Christ. The sublimity and wonderfulness of the Divine Devoid it is obedience. It went home at the orders of the kings of mysticism, metaphysics, Abrahamites descent and traditions of the divine rights of princes from being the man manifest Jesus Christ. It returns at the orders of those same dignitaries upon their humble recognition of the nameless something unreachable by any other way than through the name itself with its mysterious unction from on high, which is the redemption of Jesus Christ. He is God. It is God to be redeemed from the orders of man that he should be hidden. Redemption of conduct is unclothing it of struggle against doing wrong and of effort to do right. Security of conduct is Jesus Christ redeemed. Redemption of mind is unclothing it of fear of dangerous and trouble-breeding thoughts and of effort to think cheerfully and bravely on principle. Security of mind is Jesus Christ redeemed. Redemption of faith is unclothing it of itself. It willingly gives up its expectations. This is the last act. Letting the supreme unction of the hidden manna within the name through which it disappeared, appear again through the same way, is redemption, free grace, justification, unhidden light.

Inter-Ocean Newspaper, October 8, 1893

LESSON III

Justification by Faith

Romans 5:1-11

The eleventh proposition of mental science is that mind as the ruling principle has a right judgment as its will and meekness do agree. If a man has the will of his mind made up to conduct him through certain actions, meek listening of that will to a noble reasoning might give him better judgment than to perform as he has willed to do. A man has his neck under the yoke of cause and effect, while he is too willful to be meek or too meek to be willful. There is a meekness that is servility, because the mind has not mixed will with it. Jesus Christ said "I will" with omnipotent docility and "I am meek" with the energy of gentleness. The poise between the two is good judgment. Therefore the eleventh statement of faith in Jesus Christ is *"I believe that good judgment is Jesus Christ."*

When this good judgment is born to mind it says, like Nehemiah, *"I consulted with myself."* It says, like, David, *"My help is within me."* Good judgment makes a beautiful face and harmonious form. The everlasting beauty and youth of Jesus Christ is the eternal beauty and ever lasting charm of right judgment.

"The father hath committed all judgment unto the son." There is nothing so untraditioned as beauty. It goes by no precedents, and knows no recipes. Therefore, when Kurozumi breathed upon disease it fled and when Gasner commanded with a loud voice it disappeared. Therefore, when Eisha spoke the rain withheld itself, and when Jesus looked upon Judas he hanged himself.

The Healing Principle

You may learn many methods of healing disease, but not one will work invariably with you till you have learned the healing principle itself and found how you and it are related. The healing principle is divine will and divine meekness married. The son or formulation thereof, is perfect judgment. This heals everything that comes to it by its own method, and asks of nobody any recipe therefore. As you study the divine principle you one day must find yourself it.

There have been quarrels over methods of healing. Knowledge of the healing principle itself takes away tendency to dispute, over methods. Judgment acts coolly and calmly on the most important matters and the commonest daily transactions. One situation looks not unto Jesus Christ more stupendous than another. "All power is mine." "Pay Caesar his rightful stipend;" "Destroy me and I will remold myself." When one has touched the jacinth stone of science he feels a powerfulness, a self-respectfulness and wisdom that show him exactly how to raise a Lazarus or Eutychus. There is a way to raise the deadest man that ever was dead and a way to manage the worst situations that ever situated.

The twelfth proposition of mental science is, "Mind is self-increasing, self-strengthening, and self-informing." This covers the arrangement of the stars in their courses and the clothing of infants by the fingers of mind. Mind is able to open its gates wide as eternity and through them the glory of the nameless being flows with a light that was never yet on sea or land." The "self" is the "light." When perfect judgment is born the light of the amethyst stone transforms the world. This judgment was ordered off the planet through the name Jesus Christ and back to the planet it comes again through the same name.

Knows No Defeat

Hannibal carried a flask of poison to use in case of defeat. He was a mighty general, but he had finally to use his flask. Napoleon was always calculating what he should do in case of defeat, and met St. Helena, but Jesus Christ knows no defeat; he calculates on none, he promises none; from the first mention of his name we believe in victory, and know that even while yet the globe turns under our feet we shall see principles triumph.

After meditating upon these two themes the Apostles believed in the twelfth statement of faith, viz: "I believe that the power, within the name Jesus Christ is the name which is free grace for the world."

After talking on free grace Paul talked of glory. This was the natural expression of his mind. Everybody speaks of glory after he has spoke of free grace. *"We glory in tribulations,"* he shouted. *"We are reconciled to God." "We joy in God." "We have now received the atonement."* (Rom. 5)

The spread of your mind over your world when its illumination is great enough to see that you are justified in everything you do, say, believe, is the mystery of glorying in tribulations, crucifixions, overwork, poverty, pain, defamation of character. By the risen glory of your mind you glorify tribulations and they become delightful experiences. You shed over insults your beaming beauty of mind and they add to your luster. You gleam on the sand trenches of want, and see what charms you best in creation.

It is not the tribulations that are glorious but your quality that glorifies them out of the universe. You alone are left on the fields of contest when you have brought up from your deeps, where the shining stone of your beauty dwells, the light of your true being to shine on your world.

In Glorified Realms

In all ages men have, by certain qualities of mind been able to live in a realm more or less glorified through being able to think from their own deeps of mind. Every mind has its hidden light, hidden splendor. Whoever has brought even the least radiance from that region has been called great. He has illuminated his afflictions.

Homer thought his own thoughts, sending them forth to converse with beings of majesty described by none before him, and they kindled his words with fiery splendor. He illuminated blindness, and as long as his name touches the periods of song or story his blindness will be glorified.

The splendid diction of Milton was the astonishing of the hidden fires of the lofty themes he dwelt upon in the lonely night watch of his own uncompanioned mind, and so long as literature turns to point her finger of proud motherhood to transfixing language, Milton's sightless eyes will be the glory of her pen.

Beethoven's chords divine were chanted first in the far mountains of his own mind, and, while history sings, his deafness to discords such as unglorified tribulations surround the world with must be this glory.

"To blind old Milton's rayless orbs

A night divine is given,

And deaf in Beethoven hears the hymns

And harmonies of heaven."

To "glory in tribulations" is to live in the light that shines from within outwardly. To "glory in tribulations" according to the unmixed Jesus Christ quality within each mind is to melt the tribulations into liquid gold — a plastic substance which cures blindness and deafness and man is reconciled to life. God is life. To be reconciled to life is to rejoice in life. To rejoice in life is to see that we have the transmuting principles within ourselves which can turn all things to any form or name we choose. God is the principle of divine good. We use the principle by being one with it as the mathematician uses his principles when he is one with them.

Invisible the factor Jesus Christ; glory in translation never melts it. Milton's glory, Homer's glory, Beethoven's glory did not hold or melt away their tribulations because the actinic ray of the sun within them did not have freedom. Thus they were not reconciled to life, to God. Thus they were not at one with themselves.

To be at one with yourself is at-one-ment. There is no other atonement. Why do the unemployed millions scream today? They want to find the Jesus Christ glory that is in themselves, with which they can transmute want into plenty.

Jesus Christ as God manifest spoke plainly that he had a gospel to the poor. "Away with him!" yelled the poor. Who will tell the poor today that he whom they ordered off the planet as Jesus Christ "must come again in the same fashion?" Will any with houses in which to shelter many, many men who want work, and store-houses full of bread and meat for those who are hungry, set them at work calling upon the quality hidden within them under the name of Jesus Christ till forth from the clouds of their own mind cometh the power to make bread and wine from nothing at all but their judgments?

The transmuting glory within all men is to come out again as out of the man of Nazareth. Instead of one man I shall be all mankind. The bringing forth thereof the divinity in all mankind is all the labor there is. He who shall shelter and feed freely while the laborers are calling back in manifestations again the Jesus Christ principle in man — where is he? Man may give up the slaughter of animals for his living. The Jesus Christ principle within him being made manifest feeds him and his family without the sound of a death agony on all the globe.

He Will Come

Man may give up quarrying among the stones and weaving among the threads and call on the name of his hidden story. It will clothe him with the seamless robe and shelter him in the mansion built ages ago expressly for him and his. Do not say, "I do not believe this!" for the time is at our gates when it must be so. The years have seemed long since the sick, maimed, hungry, ordered the power of God back into invisibility through a tomb and cross. The sorrows of your lot are the tomb and cross still standing plain in your sight.

He whom ye seek will shine through them and melt them down now, today if you please.

"Call and I will come." This is the only plan by which we today can be reconciled to God. Within us is the glorifying principle. Brought forward we become by it reconciled to our life. Being reconciled to our life we are at one with ourselves. Being one with ourselves we are able to glorify our cross and tomb, which we call by the name of poverty or disease, and when these are glorified we find their places occupied by the visible fulfillment of every hope of our life.

Inter-Ocean Newspaper, October 15, 1893

LESSON IV

Christian Living

Romans 12:1-15

Golden Text: — "*Be not overcome of evil, but overcome evil with good.*"

Here is what is called a godly doctrine running its race over the religious world. It is that the divine being is subject to the indignations, griefs, and feebleness of human beings, Peloubet, whose International Texts and comments definitely express the religious concepts of our age, says: "Christ did not die to make God willing to save, he was more than willing, but enabled God to be righteous in his forgiveness." Abbott whose comments are greatly beloved by all Sunday school scholars, says: "The death of the Messiah was a revealing of the suffering and sacrificing nature of God!" Page 260 of Peloubet's notes reads: "The sacrifice of Christ was the cry of God over a lost world." There are but two or three of the emotions and frailties of mortal man left out in the modern descriptions of divine being. All that the ancient poets and priests said of Jupiter and Saturn (his father), our religious poets and priests are saying of our later deities concerning some of their incompetent or excited states of mind. Now according to the law of cause and effect it is very unhealthy, indeed, to propound nonsensical topics for consideration, and then because by opportunity the chance is offered us compel other people to consider them. The present social, financial, and political state of this world is the externalization of its religious propositions. The same propositions have been rampant for ages, whether we have set up one deity or a thousand deities as subjects of disclosure.

Now and then a proposition on the broad plan of common sense has been started out and enough people have believed in it to have a modicum of health, prosperity, and freedom manifested by almost everybody and in some cases where the godly doctrines have been well ignored a large show of health, prosperity, and freedom by some people.

Would Become Free

Gautama thought that if men would drink spring water that had stood in the sun and keep their minds dwelling on the majesty, mercy, and freedom of the Divine Being they would become free and majestic like their contemplations. Jesus taught that it would not matter so much about their drinking water if they would keep up their contemplations. Neither of these made it out that the Divine Being is in need of assistance from men, nor that he is trembling with grief or fear or anger. Zoroaster discovered as a result of his independent common sense that four classes of mankind seek out the way of illumination, buoyancy of heart, and inspiration. They are the afflicted, the poverty stricken, the seekers after truth, and the wise. On this way they drop what has been taught them and touch upon what is true. One touch of what is true and away vanisheth some measure of affliction.

Virgil believed enough in the godly doctrines of his age to have asthma so he wheezed and panted; he ignored them enough so that he sung of sweetness and fairness, of peacefulness and bravery. He ignored them so that the people rose and did him homage when he appeared in the Roman theater exactly as they rose to salute their emperor. He ignored the godly doctrines of his age so far that the poverty of his position became *non est*. There is nothing more healthy than ignoring religious propositions founded on nothingness. There is not one particle of foundation for the idea of a suffering incapable or fear stricken God or gods. We might as well speak of the principle one of the mathematics, or the principles many of the mathematics grieving over a boy's saying that they grieve, as to agree that the divine principle of the universe suffers, is angry or incapable.

Man's Co-operation

The "I" that stands back of the mind stuff can turn its thought wheels into the raw mind of material, and manufacture the kind of a life robe it chooses. I can take the word God and mix it with other words like suffering, incompetency, needing man's co-operation and the like, and fix up a million unemployed laborers in one state if I am skillfully forceful in my manufactory. If I am feeble in turning in my wheels I can do to the same by having a great many others agreeing with my proposition that God needs man's co-operation in some of his undertakings. Such doctrine of God being perpetually reiterated weaves a life robe round the planet that people rebel at.

But at the center of all mankind there stands the "I" in unconcerned, undisturbed majesty. This "I" that mixes words together and manufactures poverty, sickness, and ignorance is only the simulation of the true and uncontaminated "I."

To the contemplation of the undefiled, unresponsible central "I" turn your mind's gaze and see if it acts afraid or unhappy over your conduct or belief. Truth is as mighty as it was promised to be. You may come fearlessly up to the godly doctrines on this earth with your information that the being standing back at the center never sacrificed anything for anybody and never cried over a lost world. It is a glistening truth and down must go all preaching of nonsense where its light falls. If you are afflicted, poverty-stricken, seeking truth, or wise, you will look toward the "I" that stands undefiled at the center, for you are eager to receive of the illumination it gives by contemplation of it.

If you have gummed your thoughts to the suffering, sacrificing God described by today, you will find that smothering mass between you and the untouched "I" at the center. If you continue to ignore that mass of godly teaching handed down from the myths of polytheism, you will certainly see enough of true Being to find yourself free from your present life robe of poverty, weakness, or grief.

Be Not Overcome

The golden text of the lesson selected for today reads: "*Be not overcome of evil, but overcome evil with good.*" How many martyrs, and staunch "soldiers of the cross" that text has formulated. Each had his "good" doctrine which he said was his God's purpose, and he clubbed his neighbors faithfully for their "evil" doctrines. In modern times the clubbing is very efficient. In a town where their beautiful churches are the pride of its inhabitants they tell their merchants that unless they give such and such sums of money toward the support of their church its people shall not patronize their stores. You know how much this is practiced in your own town. It is the effort to overcome evil with good. But I say unto you that if you look toward the "I" standing untouched at the center of all things you will not be able to distinguish between the good and evil. The rain of your illumination, buoyancy of heart and inspiration will fall on the just and the unjust alike.

On every plane of social, state, or financial weaving of life robes by thoughts turning round into the obedient mind stuff out of which all things are made the conflict between good and evil is apparent.

Napoleon had woven his life place out of his mind stuff with the wheels of thought that a man may ignore birth amid the lowly and place the crown of empire on his own head. To his kingly compeers that was evil, and they surrounded him so thickly with their reminders of his inferiority that finally he accepted that word, and at 40 years of age brain and muscle succumbed.

We are surrounded thickly by the false doctrine of a suffering, sacrificing, pitying God. We ignore it; and place the crown of mastery of flesh and mind, on our own judgment.

Judgment is the uncontrolled "I" at the center. "The government shall be on his shoulders." "Of his kingdom there shall be no end." "He shall slay both the righteous and the wicked together." "His rain shall fall on the just and the unjust." "With him is no respect of persons."

Sacrifice No Burden

With unmovable judgment looking toward the unchangeable, undefilable truth we are found needing Paul's injunction to *"present our bodies a living sacrifice unto God"* (Romans 12:1). In this sacrifice we give up nothing but what we are glad to be rid of. We receive what we have been struggling for. That which never mourns stops our mourning and our causes for mourning. That which never stops our suffering and our cause of suffering. "This is our reasonable service." "Be not conformed to this world," urges Paul in the next place. We have no disposition to pick up any of the godly teachings of this world which have woven such life robes round their people. Napoleon and Virgil might pick up the teachings of religion and state and weave in defeat and asthma, but a few years experience of afflictions are sufficient for us.

We have different gifts, but they are all of one spirit, Paul says in this lesson. It is wonderful how one of us ignores one of the words of the godly preachings of the ages and another ignores another of them. What we ignore we demonstrate its opposite. One ignores the doctrine that God is good and demonstrates freedom from prejudice in favor of good people. He does not shrink from the bad nor gravitate toward the good. They are all alike to him. Of course he is not aware that he has a stomach or head after this sight of the "I" at the center which itself is not aware of such clogs and he is, without trying to do so, "presenting his body the living sacrifice" of what men have been saying was a goodly doctrine.

Knows the Future

One ignores a past, a present, and future Jesus Christ principle, and finds himself knowing the future, reading the present, speaking of the past as all one. He finds himself prophesying which

Paul here says some of us ought to be doing, and in doing this he sees no difference whatsoever between your banging the door last week in anger, and your petitioning God in agony yesterday to help you bear or take you out of your troubles. They are but emotions which the "I" at the center never experiences and he who looks at gets rid of.

"I came down from heaven now with the sight of that which was, and is, and will always be, unknowing of times or seasons" is the way the illumination of ignoring a Jesus Christ whose cause is coming, makes one present his "distributions of mercy."

Paul saw what he could see of truth from what he ignored among the godly of doctrines of his time. We see of truth what we can see after the same principle. Whether of Napoleon, Virgil, or Paul, the principle is one. What we will have nothing to do with we are free from.

We will have no suffering, pitiful, grieving God, and thus we bring to the world the ministry of buoyancy and inspiration, and have nothing to do with a being who has to be helped out of some scrape he wired himself into, we do not have to work to perform our ministry. It is the nature of that One at the center who is neither good nor evil to make you an impartial minister of health to all you meet when once you have seen that he is neither aware of evil nor good.

It is the nature of that undescribed One at the center to make you an undefilable presence in the midst of your world when you have once seen that he is neither aware of wickedness nor holiness.

It is the nature of that "I" at the center to work mighty miracles through you when you have once seen that he is not aware of anything needing to be done, and is not aware of its own ability or feebleness. Itself to itself is one.

Inter-Ocean Newspaper, October 22, 1893

LESSON V

Comments and Explanations on The Golden Text

I Corinthians 8: 1-13

Young people start out with ardent confidence in themselves, in their work, in the plasticity of matter and mind to become formulated in their purpose. They begin directly to meet people who have had great experience with the matter and mind of the universe. Those people tell them what can be done and what cannot. The young people do not at first believe them. Finally they yield first one point and then another to their predecessors and in fullness of time "go the way of all the earth."

There are two ways of receiving the accounts of men as to what can and what cannot be done. One is by consciously listening to their audible and written statements on that subject, and the other is by unconsciously feeling their mental determinations. If you become discouraged and depressed you have been taking into yourself by some means a current of the multitude's conviction that if a man or woman knowing as little as you do is as conceited as you are, they cannot possibly "set the world on fire." Heretofore you have felt almost as if you could turn the globe from east to west. Today you feel as if its law of west to east were unalterable.

Great thinkers and scholars praise Shakespeare for picturing the world and its inhabitants so accurately. He is only picturing things as men have ordained them, after subscribing to conditions. He may have expressed himself wonderfully. All the more dangerous leader for the young is he whose diction charms and enchants, whose doctrines are false.

The Estate of Man

Shakespeare tells of the estate of man as an infant muling and puling or a decrepit old idiot. Jesus tells of the estate of man as glorious in wisdom, power and ability. In the beginning now, and forever. Shakespeare describes the semblance of man. Jesus describes the real man. Jesus never yielded any point from first to last, whether the world fired its decisions at him openly or covertly. In this he ever lives as an example to the young. That which young inspiration suggested he never let go of. Thus he now lives in that presence he prophesied.

Gasner, the German genius for healing, stood boldly up before his age, and, in the presence of many witnesses, commanded the devil in the body of diseased mankind to appear and be annihilated. The devil always obeyed Gasner's order till one day Gasner's mind caught his neighbor's perpetual insistence that nobody could vanquish the devil. He let discouragement enter, and did not know how to defend himself. So he failed and, to the triumphant glee of his contemporaries, he was locked into prison and his career of usefulness ended.

Emerson continued to be courageous a number of years after he was hissed at and criticized for such unworldly propositions as that evil is negation and God is all. He finally yielded to the mental oppositions of men who had had experience enough with the world to see that there is something besides God in it and that evil is a solid lot to handle. His brain softened under the mental pressure, and he is gone out of sight like the rest.

Nothing In Self

Ruskin also continued bravely holding his own for years, but finally fell. Let all who have high hopes and great confidence in themselves stick to it. There is nothing their forceful nature prompts them to hope for but can be wrought out. If a whole race has its marshaled battalions of accounts of how impossible it is for people as slim opportunities as yours to manage destiny and a world do not believe them. Discouragement is always the first signal of your unconscious yielding. A carpenter's son snubbed and hunted, took the scepter of triumph into his own hand and by paying no attention whatsoever to the world's accounts of how the world is run, he ran it to suit himself. He took the clock of time and stopped its wheels to count the age of the stars from his birth backward. He took the laws of nature and paralyzed their angers held on the throats of empires till death and hell let go their victims, till hunger and disease slunk into kennels out of sight wherever he appeared.

"So shall thy world grow polar to thee,

Slowly taught,

And crystal out a new world

Like thy thought."

Does your expectation of your world's instinct outshine that young man's expectations? Whether it be less or greater have you yet learned how to keep yourself to yourself, shining and outshining till you have fulfilled yourself?

The Russian government is everywhere feared. Its money is almost worthless, its millions are the hungriest swarms that tread the planet but so far that nothing that the outside world says against it has ever been allowed either to be spoken within its borders or to be read. When its people hear how men regard it, its soldiers will refuse to shoot. Its women will cease to starve their babies to help furnish rubies and sapphires to line the walls of palaces. They will all slack down.

Whether a man's idea be right or wrong he holds sway with the force of it till he begins to yield to his neighbor's descriptions, either silently held or audibly told. Jesus never yielded. Neither need you yield, though you have set out to preach the gospel of miracle-working in this age of belief in old age and poverty as the unalterable conditions of the race under regular law.

What Paul Believed

Paul, in this first letter to Corinthians, shows signs of trimming his sails to meet the breezes of a world in whose actual existence he says he does not believe. He starts out by saying we all have knowledge. He says that "we know that an idol is nothing." He says there is only one God whose substance and intelligence fill everything. Then he yields a point on this by saying that "through our knowledge our weak brethren may offend; for whom Christ died."

This doctrine of our brethren being weaker than we are, and knowing less than we do, is very popular among us as ministers of Christian gospel. It is an account of our brethren which seems exceedingly plausible. As young life they started out on some plane believing they could achieve, but as a long line of priests of poverty and feebleness we have finally beaten them. Now according to Paul we must eat and drink, sleep and read in such fashions as not to complete our undertaking.

But what is worth doing is worth doing well. If the sons and daughters of Jehovah the Omnipotent can be made drunkards by our actions, but we cannot be made drunkards thereby, and the actions are nothing at all according to Jehovah, who fills them (verse 8), why should we trim sections to keep a swarm of feeble sons and daughters of omnipotence from being triumphant exhibitions of our determined descriptions of mortal weakness?

Doctrine of Kurozumi

The Kurozumi sect of Shinto have some texts similar to these texts of I. Cor. 8:1-13: *"Never take off your hat in an apple orchard." "Never tie your shoes in a melon patch."* "Why? Because your neighbors may think you are dodging to snatch an apple, or stooping to steal a melon." It is the doctrine of doing to be seen of men, which is hypocrisy, which is subtle influence on men to make them follow our hidden idea that when we are alone we will drink and eat, play cards and dance to suit ourselves.

"Wherefore," says Paul, "If meat make my brother to offend. I will eat no flesh." Yet, he admits that "meat commandeth us not to God; for neither if we eat, are we the better; neither if we eat not, are we the worse." How can he possibly reconcile telling us, "whether we eat or drink to do all for the glory of God," with advising us to eat and drink according to our "weaker brethren?" You can see for yourself that one way is to be seen of weak brethren, and another is to be seen of God, who cares not how we eat or drink. (Verse 8)

Here at the plausible grandeur of the Pauline texts, we cast off the shackles of long lines of armies agreeing therewith and proclaim on the wings of this gospel morning of Jesus Christ that there are no "weaker brethren" for whom we are to comfort ourselves, and no suspicions of our life or character can alter our recognizing that the frequenters of barrooms and the inhabitants of poorhouses are as strong and wise and good as the noblest Christian Ministry.

Ages of teaching that weakness and sinfulness are the nature of men have only made them seem to be weak and sinful; never made them really weak or sinful.

He, who can stand by this doctrine and ward off the mental convictions of the world's religious teachers will be rewarded by seeing mankind step forth in all the pristine splendor of their estate in that day when God pronounced them good.

Does the Almighty trim his actions to suit the suspicious, weak, foolish, sinful? Does the Almighty be in want, repulsiveness, and defeat? Then why should we?

Setting forth in this ministry we need not lose heart nor expect failure though we have for our inspiration the restoration of mankind to their original beauty and strength and majesty. That which whispers or shouts that it cannot be done today has forgotten Jesus.

Inter-Ocean Newspaper, October 29, 1893

LESSON VI

Science of the Christ Principle

I Corinthians 12:1-26

Martin Luther said he would rub the ears of the Almighty with his own promises till he fulfilled them. This sounded woefully sacrilegious to his contemporaries, and doubtless to the stately sanctimony of many of our own time it is making free with what should not be made free with.

Poor Paul is rubbing the ears of his own doctrines of resurrection with vigorous zeal in this (1 Cor. 12:1-26). He has never heard the statement of religious science which reads: "Act as though I were and thou shalt know I am," yet he is acting both with mind and tongue as though resurrection from the grave were a demonstrable principle, and, not only that, but had been already perfectly demonstrated by Jesus of Nazareth.

He also says that if Christ is risen, then all men may rise. He, the first fruits and all others afterward. "Then cometh the end, when he shall have delivered up the kingdom to God, even the Father, when he shall have put down all rule and authority and power."

Science of The Christ Principle

There is a science of the Jesus Christ principle. Do not stop to argue whether or not there was ever such a historic character as a carpenter of Nazareth who exhibited miraculous powers. The term Jesus Christ has come now to stand for the divinity in man. A rabbi of the Jewish church said that whether or not the Jews killed Jesus Christ, the Christians today were crucifying the Jesus Christ in man every time that it appeared.

Thinking of Jesus Christ as the divinity in man and angels, wherever there is a scientific process of studying it so as to make it absolutely manifest everywhere. If the divinity of man is not manifest it is buried behind something. That something that hides divinity is the undivine. But divinity is not dead. It is a vital spark that cannot be killed. The hiding of it is the only death there is. If you live gratifying your senses you are dead. If you live gratifying your intellect you are dead. If you live gratifying your pride of name or fame you are dead. If you live looking for praise or blame or riches you are dead. All these ways of living finally wrap an old wrinkled coat of brown and yellow flesh around you, a box of rosewood boards, and sand.

Dead from the Beginning

Resurrection for you would mean taking off the covering at any stage of the wrapping process. You are no more dead when the gravel and box hide you than when you are hidden by your struggle to get riches. The vital spark in you is the Jesus Christ in you. If Jesus, son of Joseph, took off the coat that his world tried to wrap him with, at every stage of his career he did no more than you can do even if you have wrapped a solid stone case around yourself at the invitation of the race.

The invitation of the race is all in idea. It is much wiser to dissolve the idea offered you through the air as it comes toward you than it is to accept it. There is an invitation offered you to feed your body -with dead cows and lambs. Study the science of slaughtering them and become very rich and famous. You accept it and get entirely hidden out of sight as Jesus Christ. There is an invitation offered you to study the science of slaughtering men. You study it and get rich and famous, and the Jesus Christ in you is quite hidden. There is one offered you to study the science of speech and become book-learned. Yes, do so, and hide the Jesus Christ in you exactly as much as if you studied how to blow up a shipload of men in an instant. "There is a way that seemeth right unto a man, but the ends thereof are the ways of death."

St. Paul's Great Mission

Now Paul's splendid determination to make mankind see that with the entire resurrection of man the Jesus Christ ministry would be ended has kept the idea of resurrection stinging and ringing through the air so faithfully that it is now the most alive idea that is heard inviting us. It comes against us like a fine wind. If we accept it by giving it, some attention we begin to take off our hide of flesh and intellect. If we pay all our attention to it, our whole hide out of flesh and intellect is blown off from us leaving only our vital spark in its limpid splendor, unattached to anything, unhidden by anything.

There is a way of talking and thinking which shows that vital spark. There is a way of talking and thinking which exposes the Jesus Christ in man. This way of talking and thinking dissolves the invitations of race minds to become dead. The whole mass theory is now being dissolved. The Jesus Christ in some people heretofore hidden by studying matter and intellect and exposing its melting radiance by the study of the divinity alone, they realize that their vital spark is their only substantial entity.

What The Spark Becomes

The study of it is their only study. They see that the study of money is hiding it, so they do not study money. They see that the study of art is hiding it, so they do not study art. They also see that if they see, hear, or touch anything else but it, in their daily intercourse with their world again, they get attached to the flesh pots and microbes of brain and stomach just like they were before, so they make it a principle to act as though the divine spark in mankind were the only substance of man, and by so doing they are melting and dissolving all the ideas that hide the divinity of mankind.

Wherever a pompous human being represents *in toto* the acceptance of the old invitation to gratify flesh and pride he falls down out of the sight of men. Suddenly a stream of fire from the fountain of truth melts him down. Yet not he, but his death robes, are dissoluble. We read how now there is an "epidemic of cranks, and no rich man and no notable is safe in his shoes," and nobody seems to see that it is the melting down of flesh and intellect under the limpid fires of the mighty truths that are now subtly stealing through the air, pushing the seemingly weak-minded and negative-minded and irresponsible as the readiest weapons at hand to execute the mission of resurrection or uncovering of the divinity which they refuse to have exposed any other way.

Christ All There Is of Man

That which is not true of Jesus Christ now is not true at all. The Jesus Christ in man is all there is of man. Is it true now of Jesus Christ, the divinity in man that it needs a hospital to sew up its brains or cut out its tonsils? Then it is not true that any man needs such a place for such a purpose for only that which is true of his vital spark is true of him at all.

This is an abstract principle, which if you see it as truth, will scatter the money which the rich woman is saving to found a hospital with. Finally its will melts all the hospitals out of sight. The abstract principle proclaimed vehemently by Hezekiah, slew 185,000 men in a night. One thing after another gets into the course of the abstract principles now being proclaimed through the airs and down its lips, out of sight forever, leaving the melting fire of this vital spark, unclothed to go on laying the flesh robes and mind robes of all men off, that the resurrection morning of the entire race may gleam over the hilltops today.

Divinity Manifest in Man

In the science of divinity in one statement has to be that what is not true of the divinity in man is not true of him at all. If Martin Luther had to rub the ears of God with his own promises, till he fulfilled them, and Paul had to rub the ears of the doctrine of resurrection till it compelled a world to believe in it, students of Jesus Christ must fearlessly, and ceaselessly proclaim that the Jesus Christ in man is all there is of man till everything that represents flesh, and intellect is melted out of sight, no matter what or who it is. The Jesus Christ in man must stand forth, must be exposed. The prophecies must fulfill. Under the reign of flesh, and intellect doctrine there are millions and millions of starving and ignorant human being. Under the reign of the divinity doctrine the gospel of Jesus Christ to the poor melts the hands and the bonds that hold back their rights. That kingdom must utterly cease.

Christ Principle Omnipotent

Can anything stop Jesus Christ from turning and overturning the idea that make poverty, weeping, disease, death? Can anything prevent the Jesus Christ principle from operating when it is set going? If the world ideas, which make sorrow now and hunger can be melted by truth let us proclaim truth. "We wrestle not against flesh and blood, but against the rulers of the darkness of this world."

Who disputes that it is ideas that rule the world? Have we not had the darkness of ruling ideas on the undivine side long enough to be willing to burn them up in the fires of the divine ideas? The divinity of the race now begins to uncover. It asserts itself. "Speak the word only and my servant shall be healed." Speak the word only and the mission of Jesus is fulfilled.

Inter-Ocean Newspaper, November 5, 1893

LESSON VII

The Grace of Liberality

II Corinthians 8:1-12

The times were excruciatingly hard for men as to finances and socials when Paul wrote this letter to the Corinthians. (II. Cor., 8:1-12) We are duplicating them in our own day almost identically. The Geneva version of the "deep poverty" renders "the poverty that had consumed them to the very bottom." Arnold's "Roman Commonwealth" says: "Macedonia had lost the benefit of its mines and was suffering from the weight of taxation."

Of all the early Christians, Paul got the most calumny. He had mixed himself up so thoroughly with the race delusion of necessity for strenuous exertion of mind and body as carrying on the Lord's work or any great change of sentiment toward better conditions of life that of course he got it right, and left. We got struck and scratched along the line of our toughest delusion. They called him "boastful." They said that he was "insincere and foolish." He was giving every instant of time and every cent he had and getting a bad name, but he made such hard labor of his strenuous exertion. Only feeling of its being his noble duty held him to the grindstone calumny, suffering in every fibers. Evidently he was high-strung and sensitive and spoke impulsively, often needing friendship, not criticism, and this made him seem foolish.

They called him "worldly, not spiritual," and also untutored in speech and mean looking. He had some personal peculiarities which they discussed often, and many stayed away from his services on account of them. He had a way of praising people who showed themselves utterly given to his doctrine which excited jealousy among even themselves and they also said such sharp things of him as to his personal qualities that he was an object of scornful neglect by his descent (lower) contemporaries. Yet here he is, writing these which shall outlive the memories of the ages; shall be the study of mankind long past the memory of even the names of the great of his time.

Which Shall It Be?

When a tremendous principle fires a man, and he sees that it is the highest that has been revealed to mankind, shall he practice along that highest to the best of his ability, or shall he practice along the halfway lines because he has got mixed up with them?

Paul left his law bench because he saw a principle of defense in the Christ doctrine. Paul took no pills or poultices because he saw a healing power in the Christ principle. Paul earned no money by doctrine, machine making, bookkeeping, because he saw the principle of support in and by his doctrine. When he turned to any of these things again it was always in a moment of heart faltering and discouragement, as if he were not worthy to do so tremendous work as he saw ought to be done. How often he acted as if he would like to hide his head and pray forever in secret, but one duty after another called him out again to face criticisms. Now his asking contributions has brought a terrible rebuke upon him. They said he is making it "a crafty cloak for his own avarice."

How does it happen that such heartfelt fidelity gets such whippings? Paul is only mixing himself with his own delusions. We all hold more or less of the same delusion today. It is the delusion that has yet proven the power of the Holy Ghost to act in homely daily conditions. We all seem to think we must work our heads off waiting for a power of the Holy Spirit sufficient to do all things.

If we are temperance lecturer we say we see that there is a time coming no doubt when there will be somebody with a flow of the Holy Ghost through him strong enough to stop men from opium eating and brandy drinking, but "meantime we must plod on."

That is a delusion. Stop tying yourself up in it. The Holy Ghost is strong enough in you now to do all that belongs to you to do. All that you are struggling for is humbug.

The Spirit is Sufficient

If we are preachers we say we see that there is a possibility of the power of the Holy Ghost streaming through some body strongly enough to break bread and provide clothes for the multitude, but meantime we must ask wages of our neighbors and do like the rest of the world.

There is a neutral to the sour milk of such ideas. It is the firm words, "I am not identified with delusions." Faraday's neutral to the biting acids that had eaten up the silver cup distributed them and left the clear silver in sight. Elisha's neutral to the biting sours that hid the army distributed the sour world of opinions and exposed the friendly host.

We have a neutral to the biting acid of the world delusion that has eaten up the silver and gold the shelter and uprightness of mankind. We apply the neutral and the acids scatter, leaving protected happy mankind in sight. It is our pause of utter withdrawal from all delusive teachings about "meantime operations." There is no "meantime," in the Holy Ghost. No call to the best we can, though we see a higher principle. If I see that my principle is my life I need not ask a doctor to help me live. If I see that my principle is my protection, I need not ask a lawyer to defend me from the effect of calumny or spoliation (act of plundering). Of the power of Christ's people in deep poverty Paul said he could testify and even beyond any power he expected they were able to carry on the gospel. "To their power I bear record, yea, and beyond their power."

It is to this which seemingly is beyond your power you are this moment called. Paul's fame went out as a great and powerful preacher. The calumnies never affected his name even in his own time so that he was not looked upon as a leader. The slights of his contemporaries really gave him greater freedom to speak boldly. "The action of his contemporaries" were the strike-back of his delusion that there were many things to be done before the coming of Christ. That idea is here now needing a neutral to its biting acid. There is nothing to be done before Christ gets here. All your suffering from the calumnies of people, all your suffering from the oppositions of others, is your delusion that you will do the best you know now till the Holy Ghost arrives. The fame of Paul and the rich contributions of the heavily taxed Christians show that the Holy Ghost was already there; which means that Christ was already arrived and doing all that was done.

Working of the Holy Ghost

The prosperity and noble reputation, the vitality and opportunities of the Christians in this age who have let go of their old labors, old studies, old friendships, shows that the Holy Ghost is here doing everything that is done. Now we can see how Paul need not have been stung. He had a doctrine that brought the principle of such utter independence of all things that its chief axiom is: "The more independent one is the stronger he is." What is independence? It is withdrawal of mind from delusions. And the chiefest of delusions is thus we will work along these lines we are now working in till a new influx of power arrives.

We see that the noble influx of power is here now. From our mind we let fall the idea that there is any more power for us than we now have. We are not obliged to do the best we can and try to harden ourselves against stings. We let go the delusion that we must do the best we can. The Holy Ghost has already arrived. We know nothing else. What is also free and independent as the Holy Ghost? Nobody need to be called high-strung so that he makes blunders when he hears of calumnies or is told of disasters if he is wholly turned into the Holy Ghost.

Does anybody dare say that Christ is not here now in all the uncovered splendor of his whole being? Who is willing to wrap himself in the delusive teaching that the Holy Ghost power is waiting for us to preach temperance, almshouses, mission schools, and charity clubs; while its glory is in route for our world? Every one of these ideas is a delusion of temporizing with which we must deal so long as we identify ourselves with it. We can leave it when we please and perform a truer ministry.

Not one of them is anything but the extension of our thought of waiting for the Holy Ghost to some day come in its power. Let go the whole swarm. "Come ye out from among them." What ye attend unto that ye have in your midst, Holy Ghost or criminals and paupers at choice. Let go delusions and be free from their signs now. There is no doctrine of delay in Christian science.

The more unresponsible we are at, the more we accomplish. The Holy Ghost being all, does all that is done. As it now neglects nothing we are now free from obligations. Do you know any higher doctrine than "Cast all your care on God?" Letting go all now we have all now. This is the inner meaning of Paul's eleventh text: "That there may be a performance out of that which ye have."

Inter-Ocean Newspaper, November 12, 1893

LESSON VIII

Imitation of Christ

Ephesians 4:20-32

It is natural to avoid complainers. They emit and spit depression of mind and all around them. A certain mother cautioned her daughters against associating with those who spoke of the faults of their neighbors often, because they were "cut out" for misfortune, "and nobody likes to have unfortunate friends," she said.

An occult visionist received that just below all of us is a round globe of soot-colored gas, each little flake of which is a gloomy point ready to shoot up through our feet with a subtle whisper against somebody or something. Complainers give this sooty sphere liberty to flit and spit through and into their vital parts, and it is wonderful how mice and moths, spiders, and disasters abide with those people.

The occult visionist also perceives that just above us all is a round globe of shekinah white light each little flake of which is a cheerful point ready to drop down through us a smiling whisper in favor of everybody and everything. People who do not complain let these tiny white flakes fall softly into their vital parts and it is wonderful how mice and moths, spiders, and disasters never seem to damage them or their possessions. You may tell about their faults and peculiarities, their foolishness and incompetence, but they are those elect.

"Who seem not to compete or strive

Yet with the foremost still arrive,

Prevading still,

Spirits with whom the stars connive,

To works their will."

The globe below our feet is gloom. The sphere above our head is joy. Each fluffy ball is eternally waiting to gain entrance. Let up the soft bitter soot flakes and our fellow men seem to us to be rich people paying starvation wages to employee and making presents of millions to mummy cases. Let in the soft, white flakes and they seem like the earnest people floating the air to find the way to God. Speaking from the mental science standpoint we may explain that there are no such spheres lying around. We may say that gloom and joy are generated by, our own persistent words, thoughts, opinions.

Speaking from the practical standpoint we may insist that whether generated by thoughts and expressions of thoughts, or already awaiting us, makes no difference; the fact is the same, viz., that we are happy or unhappy, sick or well, prosperous or unfortunate at our own will.

A Source of Comfort

It is a great thing to know within yourself that you are worthy of the high estimation of the whole world while you are catching the calumnies of those whom you have done good and not evil unto all the days of your life. That knowledge is sufficient to push down the gloom sphere; draw in the joy sphere, and make your very breath a health to your family.

Occult visionist or sage metaphysician, you are the chooser of your destiny, your name and your fame. You may know about your worth or your unworthy at will:

"Here eyes do regard you

In eternity's stillness.

Choose well: your choice is

Brief and ye endless."

When you begin to let in the white flakes you are willfully cheerful. This is Christ principle. When you feel the old sphere letting go its cleavage and descending downward, that principle is your life, your light, your clear mind. That cheerful turn you put upon every situation is the Christ turn of Christian science, the joy turn of mental science, the ceasing-to-complain turn of the occultist.

Paul urges it from two standpoints as the greatest principle he ever dealt with. *"Be renewed in the spirit of your mind, that ye put on the new man.* (Eph. 4:20-32) First from the mental side then from the Christ side. He makes them one. He says nothing about the two storage globes.

He makes out that to cease from lying and stealing will pull off the old man. He asks us to tell the truth about our neighbors. He ought to add plainly that it makes a difference to us what spheres are diffused through us as to what we call truth of our neighbors. One man calls the tramp in his back yard an honest man and gives him important errand to attend to which he does honestly. Another man calls him dishonest and locks his doors with spring and bolt, both of which the tramp picks open.

One says Mr. Jason's children are treacherous and need severity. Another says that you can depend upon them every time if you do not attempt severity. One says man, marriage, finance, governments are failures. Another says there is no failure. One says there is evil, terrible evil to combat. Another says "evil is delusion of mind; all is good.

What Causes Difference of Vision

On the principle of the two spheres it is plain what causes the difference of vision of different men. Paul rises to spreads of splendor, urging us to absorb new ideas and let go old ones. The occult visionist rises to radiant confidence, urging us to breathe from the white sphere and roll downward the spark sphere.

Finally we see that it is not necessary to say whether there is evil or not, because each one sees that it is himself only he is dealing with, and that self of him is neither good nor bad; it is free will.

We see that there is absolutely free choice to mix two spheres and the undivided states; to be either one or the other and complain or rejoice; to think independent of sphere and find slums and beggary, or cleanness and plenty, to mirror our thoughts. We do with ourselves and the world what we please. We preach non-resistance, believe in its success, and realize our doctrine. We preach combating of evil, violent defense of morality and find necessity for such activity at every turn.

One preaches that we live in a hollow basin, and on-the-ball principle explains getting around to our starting point by keeping straight ahead.

Each theory has sensible adherents, who look with great contempt upon other theories. Each philosophy, each religion points to its proofs. But finally it's all one in the same. We see what we have chosen to think. We deal with what we ourselves ordained to deal by our free choice. It was always so. The life principle is the free will.

Paul is talking through this chapter to such men and women as he must of necessity be forever dealing with, because back there at his free-choice point of being he was forever choosing to think about how miserably incompetent the Creator of man had shown himself.

"Man by nature is full of lust and lying!" he shouts. "He was formed that way!" "He must fight heroically against such a despicable nature!" Then Paul, who agrees that his own nature is identically the same as theirs, tells them how to fight. A good and persistent fighter sometimes tells of victory. This man seems to burn with victory sometimes and this is an encouragement to other free-will choosers of the contention principle to conduct life by.

Nothing But Free Will

But now what if all this harangue about fighting, striking, crucifying the natural man is humbug? Suppose one rises from the starting point, viz, his free choice of how to see his world, and will have no more complaining either of himself in his world? As true as he lives he will see that there was never anything or anybody to fight or train or trim or abuse.

There was never ending and there never will be anything of you but see your free choice, which is your free will. Run to mathematics with your choice and the limitless principle of the unit will go on to calculations of things beyond the sun tipped zones of Canis Major. Run the free choice to descriptions of goodness and the infinite principle of good, will string its splendors of happiness to the joys of some realm beyond words or thoughts.

Run your free choice to the terrible world and find hordes upon hordes of power of earth and powers of air creating themselves for your sake and on and on through such ages as your free will to think of such things may decree. At the end you will be just where you are now, just who you are now, and just as you are now, viz., a starting point.

There is no naturally bad person to strike into, chain down, or shoot at, either in yourself or anybody else. It is your chosen way of looking at people, yourself included. Your right of choice is your terribleness, your glory, your divinity. Knowing this to be a seminal truth, who is there still loving to insist that his surroundings are bad, his neighbors are hungry, his appetites are defiling? What made the greatness and wonderfulness of Jesus? Having chosen a base he stood there. "I am not flesh and blood only as I choose to be. I am Divinity." Nobody struck or crucified him off that premise.

He knew his worth and held to it. He knew his power and held to it. He preached deliverance to captives. There are other styles of captives besides captives of war or appetite. There are captives to doctrines. There is the doctrine of many men and women, being in pain and poverty. The doctrine keeps you tied hard to the sight of pain and poverty whether you are compassionate or hardened. But the men and women your doctrine describes never existed. They are figments of imaginations choice. There is the doctrine of many people being ignorance. This keeps you tied hard to the sight of many stupid creatures who have no actuality.

There is Paul's doctrine of sinfulness. This keeps you tied to the sight of such people as he describes. You are free to let go of doctrines and start out afresh, unattached, unmolested, unburdened with Paul's crowd, your own former crowd, any crowd, either of doctrines or persons.

Your name is Free Will to Choose, your choice is you as you were in the beginning and forever will be.

Inter-Ocean Newspaper, November 19, 1893

LESSON IX

The Christian Home

Colossians 3:12-25

David sung a thanksgiving hymn after the last giant of Gath had been slain, and one of its stanzas reads: "With the merciful thou wilt show thyself merciful, and with the upright man thou wilt show thyself upright. With the pure thou wilt show thyself pure, and with the forward (perverse) unmanageable thou wilt show thyself unsavory."

By this hymn David admits that God is principle, not personality. The life principle operates reliably whichever way you perform with it. Act frowardly and conditions will correspond. Act partly well and partly ill and conditions will correspond. That which makes this reliable correspondence is principle. Peloubet says that "nothing can so show the intensity of God's love for his people as does the fact of the infinite cost to him of their redemption." Does it cost the principle of a mathematical calculation anything when the boy figures incorrectly and then erases his numbers with more careful, attention to the Principle, if he computes badly. If Paul made up his computations of men and women as froward and perverse he must keep up figuring that way till something from somewhere informs him that his estimates call for cancellation. If he thinks men and women need reforming he must take unto himself a work of reform huge as the human pile of countless ages of birth and bad conduct. In this lesson the subject of last week is continued. Poor Paul, poor reformers, whoever and wherever they may be?

Divine in the Beginning

At their starting point all men, women, children, are divine. He who keeps his mind's eye on the starting point of mankind has nobody to reform. He sees them as they are. He who figures on mankind as undivine will have his, head, heart and hands more than full washing out slums. He has men as they are not.

The pietists of generations ago prayed for a time when the world's wickedness should be rolled away and its divinity be exposed. They prayed for Christ's coming with the power of truth. They figured on a long time ahead of them before the truth of God should reign. We are grateful to them that they did compute on an end to error. We are thankful that the calculated end has come. They would rise in wrath perhaps if told that error's reign ceases only by the pietist's ceasing to err. They might possibly agree with the present church militant that it is blasphemous to cease erring by keeping the mind's eye on the divine starting point of man and looking no longer upon him as heathen, intoxicated, or sinful. They might agree with Paul and modern reformers that we ought to look upon men and women as our minds were trained to look upon them.

But here is the doctrine that answers their prayers, whether they are pleased with it or not, "It is the truth of God, the truth of man. It has come to reign. And of its kingdom there shall be no end." Attention to it is erasure of the giants of Gath.

The four giants of the Gath of this hour are, Decay and Death, Pain and Poverty. The instant the world sees the principle that slays these giants of Gath their song will agree with David's moment of illumination: "With the pure thou wilt show thyself pure, and with the froward thou wilt show thyself unsavory. They will recognize God as principle. Then they will hold new views of man.

The pain and poverty of our world seem so tenacious because we so tenaciously cling to our former views: but the most tenacious errors finally yield to truth, so we keep proclaiming the perfect doctrine, which erases error as its name is spoken.

"In the morning sow thy seed and at evening time withhold not thy hand." "In such an hour as ye think not the Son of Man cometh."

Blessings of Contentment

Had the pietists of ages ago been satisfied with things as they are they would not have been so uncomfortable and others around them would not have been so possessed to get them out of the way. This is truth.

When Gehazl ran to meet the Shumanite woman she told him it was well with her husband, well with her child, and well with herself. The neighbors would have called her a liar. But her truth demonstrated itself promptly.

The pietists had a hot and single purpose, viz: to have truth reign over error. They fastened with melted energy their proclamation of the wickedness of the world and its need of reforming into the race mind. The race is just shaking off their mental shackles. They thought they were telling truth. The Shummanite could have given them lessons. The truth was and is and forever will be: "It is well with me and mine." "All is well." The welding-irons of the pietists should have spoken this justification of what is. It would have been watching truth instead of handling error. If God were a being to resent, to feel hurt and cast down, he certainly would have taken vengeance in those peitists who maligned his handiworks so continually. But God is principle; not blasphemable, not alterable; only usable. It is only to the revengeful he acts with revenge, only to the reformer he acts reforms. "To the pure all things are pure."

Project yourself from your free will starting point, where all is well, out over the universe and if obliged to act graciously in a quarrel Paul and you will make alliance. Forbearing ". . . if any man have a quarrel against any."

Free and Untrammeled Energy

Project your energy from its free starting point where all is well to never believed that anybody had any quarrel against you and you will not need to be either gracious or ungracious. You simply won't be there. You simply can't feel them. You keep your starting point unentangled.

Project yourself through the hard tunnel of agreeing that you must "put on mercies," "put on charity," at very terrible straits of temptations to be unmerciful and uncharitable, and you will also believe you must be on the alert to "strike while the iron is hot," which is the common way of looking at these verses of (Col. 3:12-25). "You must be on hand to put on mercy, charity, submission, love, obedience, when you feel least like it," says Paul. The perfect doctrine teaches that the Son of man cometh while you are not alert, *"in such an hour as ye think not."* The Son of man is the divinity in you. It rises and manages your hard places without your "putting on" anything. It asks no courage, no alertness, no brave effort on your part. It tells you to strike the iron till it is hot, which is said to have been Cromwell's idea of the principle of success.

The perfect doctrine must be proclaimed whether anything bad confronts you or not. Then when the bad faces you the iron is hot enough within you through much striking to burn down your giants. Even a very little hot of the iron is mighty to prevail. Gideon's army only numbered 300. They had to fight a countless host. He discharged 10,000 because they were afraid. Ten thousand of your thoughts are afraid you cannot cure decay and death, pain and poverty. He discharged 21,700 as too weak to fight. This is the number if your thoughts that cannot quite make out what the perfect doctrine is.

But 300 of your thoughts, smallest of your realm, even less than a mustard seed. In size all together, can put all the countless army of troubles to flight. They fight so easily that there is no show of a struggle. They dwell nearest your unconquerable divinity. They represent the hot of the iron, engendered by a steady attention to man at his starting point, God as he is, and no attention whatsoever to what seems externally to be truth.

In the twenty-fifth verse Paul sees that same principle that David saw. "He that doeth wrong shall receive for the wrong." But neither of them explains that it is principle of computation. They both say it is a great person sitting on a throne watching the conduct of men, cognizant if evil and good. Neither sees that if such a being were, he were unworthy our praise if he created men "good" tempted him with evil, and punished and rewarded him according to his handling thereof.

Maybe you say it makes no difference whether it is person or principle; we are happy in one line of action and unhappy in another line. It makes the difference between starting point out as free being or as overshadowed agent.

Inter-Ocean Newspaper, November 26, 1893

LESSON X

Grateful Obedience

James 1:16-27

There is one clause in James' first chapter, chosen by the international committee for our discussion to which our attention is called first: "Be swift to hear, slow to speak, slow to wrath." He means for us to be good and unprejudiced, listeners to all kinds of doctrines, slow to speak disapprovals of any of them, and sparing against our wrath against the worst of them.

The mind gets stiffened with the long holding to its own peculiar beliefs exactly as the body gets stiffened with long usage. Listening with docile attention to new doctrines limbers up the mind exactly as rest and change of exercise limber up the body.

There are certain words that open the pores of the mind exactly as our baths opens the pores of the body. One of the words that opens the pores of the mind is docility. Another is listening. You do not need to try to make these words work with your mind. They are their own efficiency. They only need expressing. Hard conditions of life represent the hard doctrines held in mind. One hard doctrine that has cramped many into decay and misfortune is the doctrine of comparison. Whoever believes in comparison has some hard condition fastened to his lot. Do you believe there is a distinction between good and evil? If you drop the belief, for it is an iron shoe too small for your foot. "There is nothing evil but to him that thinketh." Then if there is no evil, and good alone is present, what has that good to prepare itself with? How can it be called good? Thus the term good is comparally, and is not a word a free, transcendent being would use to describe his estate.

Think over this reasoning for a little while and see how limber and docile and young your mind will feel.

It suggests to the certainty that "there are more things in heaven and earth, Horatio, than are dreamt of in your philosophy." It is a doctrine. It is a high doctrine. James, the author in the book from which today's lesson is taken, says of high doctrine that "it is able to save your souls." You admit that salvations by the acceptance of a doctrine? The highest doctrine is swiftest salvation.

The Highest Doctrine

What do you wish to be saved from? Think a moment what you wish to be saved from. Gautama Buddha said that all mankind alike wish to be saved from decay and death, pain, and poverty, both, now and hereafter forevermore. Are these four diseases what you wish to be saved from? You will never be free from some one of them till you get out of the doctrine of comparisons into non-comparatives.

The most cheering and encouraging principle I know is the principle of asking up a proposition till it manifests itself. Some English and Indian gentlemen were in the habit of meeting evening after evening and mentioning the characters and works of historic mystics. One whom they often spoke of was Jesus of Nazareth. One evening Jesus manifested himself to them and spoke to them.

A writer had been night after night penning his thoughts of the angelic hosts that surround mankind. About 2 o'clock one morning, after a profound and almost ecstatic contemplation of these glorious beings, he felt a cool waft of filmy air blowing past him, and in its wake, he beheld noble and entrancing figures. Those would have remained till now invisible to those thoughtful men if their persistent descriptions had not been given forth.

On this same principle it become us to talk and think the highest doctrine we know till it manifests itself. One high proposition we must maintain forever, and that is that rag-picker is as transcendent a being as the angel Gabriel, or as Jesus Christ himself.

A Mantle of Darkness

The rag-picker's garb and thievery are the mantle of darkness thrown over his splendor by the world-wide doctrine of comparisons. Take off the doctrine of comparisons and his character, as he is known in heaven, is exposed. The man who rouses himself out of the doctrines of men sets himself and posterity free. Rouse to proclaim that the transcendent beings that circle among the air spheres near our faces are the rag-pickers, that prison convicts', the saints' divine martyrs, waiting to shine on our sight, and their mantles of wickedness will fall. Swedenborg saw that the angels gazing on the faces of men see only beauty and holiness pictured forth alike, from the black and the white, the sinful and the righteous. What right have I to see the street crowds or gaunt wanters? What right have I to see 2,000 waifs of misery? Is not more an evidence of my being bound up in the doctrine of evil and good, in comparison, than of my freedom in truth, if I watch the hosts of heaven speeding now over our globe, and give you reports of their misery?

Which way was it my duty to speak and write of the beings I meet if I know that the way I speak and write of them they will manifest plainly? Paul said he had not shunned to declare unto men all the counsel of God. What is the counsel of God concerning my neighbors take of God, who sees them truly, counsel me to make up a way of seeing them either to suit myself or the race of error?

Now, who shall say the lily is dark because the night is dark on its face? Has the sunshine changed the lily? When truth shines on the squalid dens, are they squalid dens then? If the lily is the lily night or day, so home and happiness are eternally here whether I lie around them or not. So you are an angel of light and beauty whether I call you by your right name, describing you as you are, or lie about you.

The Counsel of God

Jesus Christ said: *"Let the dead bury the dead."* James says here in verses 23 and 24: "For if any be a hearer of the word, and not a doer, he is like unto a man beholding his natural face in a glass; for he beholdeth himself, and goeth his way and straightway forgotteth which manner of man he was."

This means for an instant while you are being told of your spiritual and divine greatness you agree that it must be so both with all men and your own self. This is the counsel of God. Then you mix among the dark descriptions painted by reformers, missionaries, philanthropists, preachers, newspapers, and straightway for it, what manner of men able here among us. You must not step out of the truth. You must do with your world as though they were as they are.

Begin with your own family. This is the unit. Believe in their nobility, their greatness, their wisdom, their hearts, their beauty. Never cease believing in them. From them it will slip out to the world. There is a reason for your hope of them. Then, finally, seeing them as they are all over the planet, you will see no evil to compare the good with, and you will find a world where another quality begins, unknowing of good and evil exalted out of their reach.

"If any man boast let him boast himself the God of Truth." Can we tell a too wondrous story of what is going on here in our midst now?

Notice the twenty-fifth verse, "*Whoso looketh into the perfect law of liberty. And continueth therein, shall be blessed.*" If you look into the perfect law of liberty, you will see there that all inferiority comes from an openness of mind to receive the wandering, bodiless thoughts that are passing through the mental atmosphere. They tell of some being born with small intelligence and some with large intelligence. Whoever receives these bodiless thoughts takes one or the other side of the question and shows weakness or strength of mind. But he was and is something quite different from either side of the question. He is a free being, so free that he may clothe himself with weakness or strength and in that garb appear to his world; but he is neither weak nor strong; he is himself.

Blessed Beyond Speaking

To know this is blessedness. To continue to regard yourself as independent of your inferiority or superiority, of your goodness and badness, is blessedness beyond speaking.

The greatest freedom comes from unclothing yourself of your idea of the world. Your idea of God is not God. Your idea of man is not man. It is perfect rest of being to let go of the idea of God and the idea of man. Ideas are heavy luggage. You are not under obligation to have any ideas. You are better off without them. This is the perfect law of liberty. Set free by it, you do not see men as candidates for jails. You do not see children as prone to fall into temptations. You do not see savages and heathens needing missionaries. You do not see sick and dying men and women. You see their unhidden soul. One sight of undarkened soul is sufficient. From that one sight which you give them they come into freedom.

Do you know any teaching diviner than that soul is not cumbered by good and evil; soul is unspoilable liberty?

Inter Ocean Newspaper, December 3rd, 1893

LESSON XI

The Heavenly Inheritance

I Peter 1:1-12

Peter speaks of the elect of God as if they were according to his foreknowledge, and those not elect are implied as also according to his foreknowledge. God he describes as the Father of all. Thus God, the Father, originated the saved and the unsaved, if we read the text outwardly. But the scriptures have been acknowledged to have both an outward and an inward significance. As the outward text is not satisfying to the soul nature, we will look to the inner text.

"He that is identified with me sitteth in my throne." Whose throne? The throne of that principle the thinker, the worker along any line has so identified himself with, that when his name is spoken the name of the principle he proclaimed is remembered also.

One would think the principle of the Archimedean screw began with Archimedes, so identified is he with it. One would think that justification by faith began with Martin Luther so identified is he with it. The doctrine is not mentioned without remembering him, and he is not mentioned without remembering it.

How high a principle are you identifying yourself with that you may not be distinguishable from it. Jesus Christ sits on the throne of the Father through making himself one with the Father. One could almost get the idea that there never was any saving love till Jesus came, so identified has he become with saving love. One could almost believe there were heathen to be lost if not knowing of Jesus Christ, the historic character, so has the knowledge of the Jesus Christ principle been brought to light by the Nazarene.

Suppose we identify ourselves with the principle of letting the dead bury their dead, and of never wrestling against material transactions, but rather attending entirely to the rulers of the darkness of the world as they sit upon their shadowy thrones in the mental ethers.

"For we wrestle not against flesh and blood, but against principalities and against powers, against the rulers of the darkness of this world." This is the same as "Let the dead bury their dead." It means that while we fight hand to hand and sword to sword with polygamy it will still flourish; while we fight hand and head and neck against rum it laughs with glee; while we fight rich corporations with strikes, we, the strikers, starve and the corporations hide their gold.

In the realm of the outward there is a law of deity on the side of the heaviest artillery, but this outward law is only the shadow flung athwart space by that eternal principle regnant in the mental universe, viz., that the heaviest artillery be in the mental universe, and let the outward and material fall into line as it best can. Shall we then be doing any different from Jesus Christ's practice and teaching!

Message to the Elect

"To the strangers to this doctrine scattered throughout the kingdoms and republics, elect according to the foreknowledge of God, grace unto you" This is the message: As the same spirit is in you all you are all by it elected to dominion over the darkness of this world, whose name is decay, death, pain, poverty, through identifying yourself with your own spirit which Peter calls Jesus Christ.

You identify yourself with that principle which puts out darkness by never occupying your mind with anything different from it.

If you say, "I must attend to my children's suppers," you are identifying yourself with the supper principle, and by being faithful to it you will sit in the throne of supper or no supper, according to your rallying energies in meeting cost of coal and eggs. But if you say, "I watch for the word of truth that feedeth the word, and I speak boldly," you are identifying yourself with the Jesus Christ principle, which is able to show you a table spread for your family and all nations together in the house of God here in our midst.

"He spreadeth a table before me in the presence of mine enemies."

"That thou seest, that thou beest." If the leader of a children's choir flats on some notes the best singers among those children will hear that flat, and hearing will imitate. Some choir leader has taught us long to flat on the high notes of the anthems of Jesus Christ. Let us leave him on that theme and sing truth. If we see Jesus Christ as a man hanging on a cross suffering and arranging to help the world out of hunger and trouble in some far off age, we will leave that flat principle and sing Jesus Christ as the fearless and triumphant principle in all mankind equally present.

If we have flatted out on the high tone that if Jesus Christ in man is never hungry or in prison or on a cross or mourning over deferred homes nobody ever has, we will sing boldly out from the welled up music of our childhood's harmonious truth that only the son that dwelleth secure and joyous in the mountains of light is alive or hath voice or speaketh or is present. On this principle look at verse 9: "Receiving the end of your faith, even the salvation of your souls." What is the salvation of the sun in the heavens from the darkness that surrounds it? Is it not making the darkness nothing and exposing the sun as it is?

"The end of faith," here meaning the final of our attention to our principle, is it not identification with the principle we attest unto?

Not of the World's Good

What clouds and darkness hide the triumphing sunshine of the Spirit in man? Only his taking up with the principles that claim to be Christ Jesus but are not Christ Jesus. Jesus Christ, equally present in all men everywhere without distinction if race, color, or previous condition, is not identified with the world's good. The world's good is its charity, its culture, its religion.

When the world visits the sick in charity is it visiting Jesus Christ or the sick?

"When saw ye me sick and visited me?" When the world's charity preaches to the prisoners sees it Jesus Christ, the triumphant and unprisonable, or roughs and toughs and tramps? "When saw ye me in prison and visited me?"

When the world studies books and dissects animals for its high culture is it getting its lessons in instantaneous instruction in languages from the fountain of knowledge where all is one wisdom and goodness? "Learn of me." Thus with the rulers of darkness the Spirit in man is not identified.

When religion teaches that here and now is our chance for safety of soul or we shall be everlastingly too late, with that doctrine the spirit in man, equally glorious everywhere, hath nothing to do.

"Whether shall I flee from thy presence? If I make any bed in hell thou art there." Though, we have identified with the death-and-hell principle, yet we may sing out of it.

This is the fearless principle; this is the victorious principle, with which, if your mind identifieth itself, it shall sit in the throne thereof regnant over trouble and hardship. The doctrine of the spirit is all about spirit. "Wherefore," says Peter, "gird up the loins of your mind for the grace that is brought unto you through the revelation of Jesus Christ." It is now the acceptable time for the Jesus Christ principle to reign. "Whoever hath identified therewith cannot be distinguished from it. "He that is identified with me sits in my throne."

Inter-Ocean Newspaper, December 10, 1893

LESSON XII

The Glorified Saviour

Revelation 1:9-20

There have been men and women on the earth who have felt peculiarly called by the divine law to step out from their common-place tasks into strange pathways.

David was called from taking charge of sheep to the priestly kingship of Judah and Israel. Joan of Arc was thus mysteriously guided from the farm to the battle field. John, the fisherman, left his nets and preached to the Kingdom of God according to Christ Jesus.

There is no telling how miraculous might be the ministry of one who has entirely left behind him his former thoughts as he left behind him his former trade. It was formerly the custom for men to believe it meant martyrdom or stupendous abuse to step into the pathway of service of the Spirit of Light and Life. John took this thought with him when he left his fishing boat and never let it go till he was boiled in oil.

The next round of ministers of the omnipotent principle called Jehovah will have learned wisdom from their predecessors. They will see that their experiences will tally with their ideas. Dr. Dulles called disappointments "his appointments," meaning that disappointments of the Lord of Peace and Freedom. That is a private opinion lugged along into Christian ministry which thousands upon thousands have groaned under. "I offer you cold and hunger, rags and death," is the Christian war call.

Self-Glorification

John starts out his lesson with self-glorification, that this opinion brought out from the tomes of ages and agreed to by himself has worked so well. Revelation 1:9: *"I John, who also am your brother and companion in tribulation."* He keeps it up through the whole book of Revelation. He makes very little account, consciously, of the principle plainly enunciated By Jesus Christ that the Lord of life and strength is a servant of man, not a hard eternity-waiting taskmaster. Through the outward text of this lesson, however, it gleams like the light of a realm that cannot be much longer hid from view that the Spirit is the servant of man, not his slave-driver. "He that is greatest among you, let him be your servant."

There is a time-old vision manifesting itself anew to a few who have thrown off the yokes their teachers tried to fit upon their shoulders. It is a vision which visited men sitting in the doors if their tents on the plains of unhistoried Egypt. It only comes to a certain kind of mind. It comes to all who are free enough to see it. Above them, within hailing distance, they see their own form, glowing, rosy, light, free, strong, beautiful, it always smiles, it is always kind, it is forever wiser than their highest conceptions, and forever out of the reach of earthly tribulations. They who have been bold enough to address their own uncontaminated self as it smiled down upon them, have found no request unheeded, no task out of its reach to accomplish for them. It accompanies us all; it is callable; it is our servant because it is our spiritual body; of which Paul spoke, which being greater than our natural body, freer, abler, serves the natural man with great service.

The All-Powerful Name

Shining upon it is a name which empowers it, furnishes its light, warms and invigorates it perpetually, exactly as some mysterious principle renews and heats the sun that lights our planet. So the name is finally our real servant, though to the visionists the rosy, buoyant presence of his own spiritual body has been so helpful that he has given it all the credit.

There have been those who asked it to carry out what would seem impossible tasks, to set aside some seemingly insurmountable difficulties, and it has brought miracles from the East and news from the West to bring to pass their requests.

Had they believed in it as some terrible task master bringing in its light cold, hunger, rags, death, they might have stayed shaded by their beliefs from its willing services to this day; but they called upon it as upon their own soul, and, like the wonderful ministry of the soul of man, it helped and wrought out tasks for them which their neighbors called miracles.

If it has been much shaded from you perhaps you cannot call it at once. But it is nigh even at your gates. Whenever by some truth John, the revelator, uncovered its presence he seemed like one in a trance of joy. Through his belief in evil and terrible dispensations its voice came colored with sounds of words which to the free mind it never uses. It was thunder to the multitude when its voice called Jesus its beloved son. It was pictures of the prophetic times to John. It would be responses of kind offers to work out miraculous undertakings for one who would be as devoted to it as John, but who would never throw up any calcium lights of insistence that awfulness and horror are the destiny of the ministers of truth.

Message to the Seven Churches

John heard it speak by symbols. He told the seven churches they were seven candle-sticks holding right doctrines. The only shreds of right doctrine those candle-sticks held were the separated sentences where evil and misery were not made out to be manufactured products of the Divine Being, which his bond-slaves, the ministers, were to undo. Now and then the present help and protection of the Divine Being are mentioned. This is truth. Thus the seven churches did some shining. John's spiritual double had some beauty and majesty, as much as his calcium lights would let be made manifest. It told as kind and merciful things as could get through such a mentality as John's. "I am the first and the last." The spiritual body is first, it is still alive when we have turned so entirely away from it that we have been covered by moss and rosewood. We may incarnate, and reincarnate again and again, always glued to our insistence upon misery as the native inheritance of man, but the smiling freedom of our spiritual body never leaves it while the life-giving name endures.

"I am he that liveth and was dead." It being hidden by thick mis-statements as to its mission and character may be called dead. It will show that it is high service waiting to speed for our prosperity, health, and joy, any time we are free enough to tell the truth about it.

The Voice of the Spirit

"The angels of the seven churches" are the true words about protection, life, inspiration, rosy joy, which the churches have let slip between the thick darkness of their theories of the horrible character of the spiritual man whose greatness and glory are the ineffable same that rusheth through the universe.

He who watches for the name finds himself turning towards his own self. It is rushing through him and through all things. He is stilled in speech and stilled in thought. His spiritual body then has entire freedom to take up its abode in him. To the spiritual man the name is visible; its power is understood by him.

The spirit of the voices saith: "Write the things thou hast seen, and the things which are and the things which shall be hereafter." We are never self-convicted of truth till we have written all that we have seen and what we believe. Then its reasonableness or unreasonableness is clear. We have one thing still unwritten on the pages of the books of the so-called wise of the earth, and that is that man has a servant willing and able to do for him all that he needs done this day, and that servant is the spirit acting by the power of a name known now upon the earth as Jesus Christ.

Its light is rising, its warmth is diffusing, its freedom is breaking over many among us. They feel the spiritual body transfusing and invigorating their natural body till there is no natural body holding sway anymore. They know that the spiritual body can speak the ineffable name, and that it is by speaking it that its eternal strength and beauty are kept. They know that their spiritual body is Jesus Christ. He is their servant, not their taskmaster.

Inter-Ocean Newspaper, December 17, 1893

LESSON XIII

A Christmas Lesson

Matthew 2:1-11

There is answering responding principle in the universe, whereby if any man or woman or child will ask a question, an answer is surely vouchsafed. Gautama Budhha asked of the responding principle, what was the cause of all the misery he witnessed, and it replied: "Ignorance: teach men truth and they will be free from misery." If the answering intelligence spoke truth the world has made slight advancement in knowledge since Gautama's date, for misery is nearly as rampant now as then, judging by appearances.

Gautama arose from his questioning and went about seeking that truth which could set free. A young man asked Jesus what he should do to be more at peace in his mind: "Sell all thou hast and be generous in giving money where nobody will know you have given," replied the responding principle.

There is no melting furnace into which money can be thrown with such insidious, subtle returns in happiness, as giving where nobody can praise us for giving. Jesus Christ knew this law well. The young man, probably had done large endowing of universities, or bathhouses and his mind was in the public papyrus reading corners, till he was restless.

A beautiful heart wished to help the hungry of the city. She went to a furnace fire and threw into it bread, with the message to it that by that it all must be fed. Within a day the newspapers noted that there was more food contributed to the poor of that city than could be disposed of. That is the breaking of bread Jesus Christ and Elisha taught, viz., use what you have scientifically, according to the spiritual method, right where you are, and see how nature will carry out your directions. What the spirit decrees nature must perform.

"Breathe Californian spices,

Roll, blue Pacific waves,

Here open the paradises.

Here close for us the graves."

Responding Principle Lives

Devout men had asked for a saving doctrine, to be preached by a man who should practice dominion over nature. "We expect him soon," said Plato. "He shall be a man of Judea, said the books studied by signs and symbols saw a star that told them, "He is here!" Their questioning had been answered.

The responding principle still lives. It was before Abraham and will be forever. The freer the mind that asks questions of it the freer the answers will come, for it is itself the free principle, and that one most free who inquires at its shrine will understand best when it responds. If you are free enough, so that you are not moving or standing still because somebody else in the universe would be grieved or angry if you did otherwise, you will be sure of a quick reply to your questioning. If anybody is fearing to move or not move lest you be angry or grieved at their doing, you are not any freer than you would be if you were tied to another's wishes. The end of the chain clasped around the slave's ankle is caught to the neck of his master. You and the free principle are not unified enough so that you hear the answers readily.

Principle is free to be the inventor's skill in making a lock, and free to be the skill of the picker of the lock; but it never gets tied up and clogged or ended in its skill where the inventor and the lock picker stop. Its skill along either lines goes ad infinitum. There is nothing like being one with the free principle. It is progressing skillfulness for ever and ever. Your money seems to be tied up to a certain amount, but if you are mentally free enough that money will replenish and multiply itself by the breaking open touch of your enchanted fingers.

Principle Not Hidebound

Principle is not tied to five plus two equals seven. It can make the nickel and copper open like pea pods and disclose pieces enough to supply 5,000 men besides women and children. This is Jesus Christ doctrine. Principle is not tied to the punishment of the wickedness. The thief on the cross felt the dry husk of his years of crime burst and scatter to nowhere when one glance of his recognition of the paradise of the free Jesus shot forth. This is free grace, viz. sudden setting free from natural consequences. Principle is not tied to the scales of old age. One glance into its unhitched speed would break off the shackles of ages. This is free grace by the sight of free truth.

How greatly are you to expect the free principle to do for you? Alexander was proud that one of his retainers asked so largely of him. Free principle feels your oneness with it if you ask it to break the shells of your meager possessions and expose to your sight now multiplied and multiplied they are, back of their crackly gateways. It laughs when you look for it to still the bondages of time to fly with it on the wings of eternity. There is no limit to its outwardness of bounty. John asked for a new heaven and a new earth right here among men. "No pain, no crying, no cold, no discouragement," he said. And he was answered that so it should be. "Put it in the time far hence," he said, and the principle let him stop ages ahead of his *anno domini* (Latin: "In the year of the Lord"). Do you put your expectations of the exposure of happiness ahead of you present? Do you suppose the free onward principle feels you are as one with it as if you expected the sight of your replenishments today with further and further exposures of multiplies so long as the sun shall shine, unstinted, young forever, the scales broken off the things that the kingdom nigh each object you touch can show?

All that is possible to be reproduced through the ages is now here. "It was here in its plentifulness before ever it appeared upon the earth," says the spirit. The ways of exposing bounty, beauty, and peace are not by the action of matter on matter but of mind with mind.

They Were Not Free Minded

The theological students at Gilgal were not free minded enough to break open the seals of the meal and see the virtues within it which free-thoughted Elisha could see. The best of the students of Jesus could not see the bread loves folded within the bread loaves, but Jesus could break the outer scales and show what multiples lay back of them.

Everything has its doubles and trebles within its bosom. Nothing needs to go through the ground, the mills, the ovens to be exposed. The mind that sees this principle as true is free. It is not tied to a process. To the bread, the wine, the clothing, the gold, of that mind Jesus often is nigh and opens increase for him though his eyes may beholden from seeing that it is Jesus. Many a time we think it was luck or extra exertion on our part that replenished and renewed or altered our goods when it was Jesus walking with us and our eyes were holden joy, reason of our being tied in mind at a stake on the highway of some principle which would not stop with us. We were set free on one line and something multiplied; tied on some line and something was holden.

They who are free from many lines, knowing that their own body is able to break open its husky shadow and expose their own majestic divinity are the "Wise Men of the East." They look daily and hourly for miracles. In the bootblack Jesus is hidden. They know they have a right to see him already born in that manger. They know it is their own tarrying while the free principle runs that hides their sight of God in the conduct and countenance of the bootblack or car driver. They know that the corn and the wine of earth being broken open by the star of truth shining with a doctrine of freedom to which they agree, will feed and revive all men that wait for better days to dawn on this earth. Herod, the doctrine of waiting till some future time for the Christ to manifest by shelling open the corn grains and the bodies of men, cannot stop this teaching that there is no limit now to the replenishing power of all things by the agreement with free truth.

He who sees that in himself is Christ; sets free some bounty of some of his goods. He who sees that in himself is all the power of Christ set free some bounty of the goods he holds with which to feed the people, clothe and beautify them. He who sees that there is no limit to his own miracle-working spirit unties himself from that stake where he once stopped speaking high principle, and thousands and thousands of miracles spring up in his wake. To him the body of Christ is manifest in every house. He falls prostrate with gladness, and from out his meager goods he multiplies and replenishes "gold, frankincense, and myrrh." He asks the omnipresent Father, "How much can I do today toward manifesting the bounty of God?" and the responding principle makes audible answer, "All things."

Inter-Ocean Newspaper, December 24, 1893

Lesson XIV

REVIEW

The hope of praise and the dread of blame being about equally balanced in one mind cause it to be good at connivance and contrivance. All connivance and contrivance is subtlety. All subtlety is Satan, who says tenderly to hope of praise or dread of blame: "Ho, nay you shall not die; you have a right to live," to such hope or dread God proclaims "Thou shall surely die."

All the lessons of the last quarter represent the struggle of hope, and dread to live their day out by claiming hope of heaven and dread of hell as commendable in mind. This is subtlest of all subtlety, since there la no hell to dread and no heaven to hope for, only as mind fabricates such places.

"I sent my soul out through the universe,
Some letter of the after life to spell.
And by and by my soul returned to me and answered,
'I myself am heaven and hell.'"

The "I" that uses its soul to go out and in among the spaces and places of eternity had better unwrap itself from all information now and then and take notice of itself. Each "I" will find itself so independent of hope and dread that it will play with those fictions no longer.

Each "I" is the author of its own experiences on the human platform and every other platform it chooses to operate upon. In the parable of Samson we see how we may take our strength and throw its energy into any receptacle we please. Samson threw his strength into his hair. The sentence that confirmed it was, "My strength is in my hair." He seemed not to be aware that he might withdraw his strength from his hair unto himself again. He therefore thought he had been shorn of strength when his hair was removed. He mourned his mistake of letting his hair escape him. This caused blindness. But the "I" of him, being the author of its own strength, made no mistake in letting a mass of hair go free. Samson being blind with his hair grown, thought it too late to use his strength again to any advantage. This was death.

It Is Never Too Late.

He who uses the sentence, "It is too late," stands at a locked gateway. He who uses this sentence would never use it if back of it were not another sentence he once used, which reads, "I made a mistake." This gateway leads to the omnipotent words, "My strength." There is one language only to which these locked gateways will open. It is the tongue of the spirit. Let him that stands saying, "It is too late," say "It is never too late with the spirit." Let him that stands saying, "I made a mistake," say "The spirit never makes mistakes." Here he touches the sentence into which he first pushed his strength. The "I" is clothed with language. Its only robe is language. He who says "my strength," discovers what sentence he pushed the strength into that he purposed to use for human encounters. Then he is master again.

The Jesus Christ doctrine is for the purpose of opening the gateways behind which we have locked ourselves. It is one in determination, viz.: to lead us back to our "I". There we hope for no praise, we dread no blame. There we are free. There we authorize our strength to go and energize, or cease where we decree.

Paul was instructing himself how to get back to his free "I" in the first lesson of this quarter. As this is review of the last twelve lessons we will notice their twelve instructions on traveling back from environments to the unenvironed "one". You will notice that unless you are able to touch the springs of an easier pathway than the scripture texts describe, as to their letter, you have the same shrinking from the Christian walk that you ever had; the same mind of expecting no great assistance in your daily affaire; but with the right key you enter the first gateway on the path of Christianity expecting an entirely new influx of light and power with which to swing your human lot more to your liking.

The Just Live by Faith

Paul said, *"The Just shall live by faith."* (Romans 1) The sentence, "I am just," will breed self-confidence. This is mental bread. Nothing brings such demonstrations of plenty to a man as the self-confidence which came out of the language, "I am just." He takes nothing from his neighbor without giving equivalent. He gives nothing that is not returned. His mind is poised. He who connives and contrives to get on in this world must get back to his "I" by the language of the spirit concerning the necessity for "managing," and the two-leaved gateway of hope and dread. He who is afraid of failure or loss has his straight way back to himself by this pathway.

In Romans 3, Paul teaches free grace and justification. It is here shown that one may speak the language of the Spirit so powerfully that his mistakes count for nothing. His human trials disappear, as though oiled out of sight. What would seem heinous offenses become instantly nothing. He heals diseases, he comforts and prospers the unfortunate whether his pious co-laborers think he has a right to or not. All of a sudden he has hit the right spring and stands free as his masterful starting point. The secret of Jesus is his at once. Martin Luther once felt his heart burn with this feeling of justification. The name Jesus Christ spoken in the heart will lead to it on one of its rounds of action. The recognition of the spirit of God equally present in all men will bring it, "God is not only in me but in you."

In Romans 5, Paul says that *"when we were yet without strength Christ died for the ungodly."* When Samson was without his strength, his strength being alive slid kindly into his hair again, since he had once started it that way. "Whenever strength appears to be what it is not it is dead. It dies for our sakes; which means that it appears to be what it is not that we may use it again. Health is not in pills, but it seems to be there. Life is not in matter, but it seems to be there. Prosperity is not in goods but it seems to be there. These are names of Christ, prosperity, life, and health is in the "I" at our starting point. Thrown out into externals they go through them first to last faithfully. Claiming that the externals are our life, health, strength, prosperity is the only ungodliness there is.

In Romans 12, Paul says, *"Bless and curse not."* Complaining is cursing. Scolding is cursing. Back of twelve gates of hiding we push our good by scolding and complaining. We enter as into his gates with thanksgiving and into his courts with praise. "At destruction and famine thou shalt laugh." If your house burns down, praise God. If the baby has the croup, praise God

In I. Corinthians 8, Paul says: *"For neither if we eat are we better; neither if we eat not are we the worse."* Here he is speaking of the "I" that remaineth the same, though its sentences folded around itself make it seem externally sick by overeating and dead by under eating. It is by speaking of the uncontaminated "one" at the canter that we show the same perfect health no matter what we eat. Christian science teaches us to speak of the uncontaminated "one" at our starting point till we manifest it in everything,

An Eternal Offer

In the fifteenth chapter of the same book Paul says: *"If in this life only we have hope in Christ, we are of all men most miserable."* Here he is speaking of our everlasting opportunities of starting at our "I" again by our use of Spiritual language. No matter where we arrive after laying off this flesh as it now looks, there on that shore we will find the same energy in spiritual language. "Let us take with us words and go unto our God." He who says words count nothing expects little from noble doctrines. He therefore speaks ill of lofty sentences. He who sees that language is Jehovah. God walks on the winds of high themes close up to his central, omnipotent "I". The chance to do this is an eternal offer.

In II Corinthians 8, Paul says: *"That there may be a performance also out of that which ye have."* What do we have? Power, light. We may perform with powerfulness and lighten the world's burdens. The light is able to draw up the oak trees and the mountains with ease. We, beginning at our all-owning, unburdened "I" center, find all performances in our world springing forth, as it were, from a new earth. The doctrine of light is the doctrine of power. The "I" is care free. It is the 'care free' who do most in this world, as the care free bones of Elisha brought the man back to life, as the care free baby in your home supports your family. Ye have care free God. The more care free you show yourselves the more Godlike ye perform. The spirit is care free, therefore it saith, *"Cast all your care on me."* In Ephesians 4, Paul says: *"Forgive."* This means, "give for." There where Samson said he was weak he should have given himself strength. He had a plenty to give. There where you say is your poverty you must pour in plenty. You have plenty to give. All things start from the all-owning "One" at our center. In Colossians 3, Paul says: *"Wives submit yourselves unto your own husbands . . . husbands love your wives . . . children obey your parents."* He is here enjoining outward and external actions. He believes that good conduct trains the mind. Others believe that good thoughts train the actions. "Whichever way we are preaching interferes nothing with the unchangeable "one" which we are in truth. James says: "In pure religion we keep ourselves unspotted from the world." He sees all external man acknowledging the uncontaminated divinity back of it. This is religion. According to this it is irreligious to see poor people or sick people; we ought to see their undefiled divinity. So Christian science is the pure religion, for it urges the divine nature of man as his real nature and dismisses his undivine nature as unreality and illusion.

Freedom of Christian Science

Peter said: "The angels desire to look into the teachings of the Holy Ghost." These teachings are the twelve high themes of Christian science, which being spoken, come facing us up with the hosts of light who are here waiting to transform the world at our word. They can transmute hardships into freedom. They can transform darkness into sunshine. They are "my servants that wait on my word."

John speaks of the greatest servant of all, namely, the spiritual "I" which is our Jesus Christ nature. Sometimes Jesus Christ seems to be without us, then again within us, as it is written: *"Jesus entered into the temple;" "Jesus went out of the temple."* In Rev. 1, John describes his idea of his helper. It is plain that an un-contaminated idea of Jesus Christ would manifest a diviner visitor.

Matthew says that Herod sought to slay the child Jesus. Herod we know is that trait in our mind which keeps us waiting for "I" to manifest health. It is that sly thought that keeps saying, "I think I must wait and go through a few more experiences before I get happy." It is that trait which makes us think we cannot have bread till we buy it, or cannot have money to buy bread till we earn it or somebody gives it to us. The Jesus Christ in us says; *"I can supply you right there where you are this moment, I am the miracle worker."* Herod quality says within us: "I would like to believe in miracles, but I can't.

The last lesson of the review is this triumphing doctrine, namely: That the true being of man is God, who knows nothing of evil or good, who is beyond description whom to know is to be like.

Inter-Ocean Newspaper, December 31, 1893

Notes

Other Books by Emma Curtis Hopkins

- *Class Lessons of 1888 (WiseWoman Press)*
- *Bible Interpretations (WiseWoman Press)*
- *Esoteric Philosophy in Spiritual Science (WiseWoman Press)*
- *Genesis Series*
- *High Mysticism (WiseWoman Press)*
- *Self Treatments with Radiant I Am (WiseWoman Press)*
- *Gospel Series (WiseWoman Press)*
- *Judgment Series in Spiritual Science (WiseWoman Press)*
- *Drops of Gold (WiseWoman Press)*
- *Resume (WiseWoman Press)*
- *Scientific Christian Mental Practice (DeVorss)*

Books about Emma Curtis Hopkins and her teachings

- *Emma Curtis Hopkins, Forgotten Founder of New Thought* – Gail Harley
- *Unveiling Your Hidden Power: Emma Curtis Hopkins' Metaphysics for the 21st Century* (also as a Workbook and as A Guide for Teachers) – Ruth L. Miller
- *Power to Heal: Easy reading biography for all ages* –Ruth Miller

To find more of Emma's work, including some previously unpublished material, log on to:

www.highwatch.org

www.emmacurtishopkins.com

WISEWOMAN PRESS

1408 NE 65th St.
Vancouver, WA 98665
800.603.3005
www.wisewomanpress.com

Books Published by WiseWoman Press

By Emma Curtis Hopkins

- *Resume*
- *Gospel Series*
- *Class Lessons of 1888*
- *Self Treatments including Radiant I Am*
- *High Mysticism*
- *Esoteric Philosophy in Spiritual Science*
- *Drops of Gold Journal*
- *Judgment Series*
- *Bible Interpretations: Series I, thru XII*

By Ruth L. Miller

- *Unveiling Your Hidden Power: Emma Curtis Hopkins' Metaphysics for the 21st Century*
- *Coming into Freedom: Emily Cady's Lessons in Truth for the 21st Century*
- *150 Years of Healing: The Founders and Science of New Thought*
- *Power Beyond Magic: Ernest Holmes Biography*
- *Power to Heal: Emma Curtis Hopkins Biography*
- *The Power of Unity: Charles Fillmore Biography*
- *Power of Thought: Phineas P. Quimby Biography*
- *Gracie's Adventures with God*
- *Uncommon Prayer*
- *Spiritual Success*
- *Finding the Path*

Watch our website for release dates and order information! - www.wisewomanpress.com

List of Bible Interpretation Series with date from 1st to 14th Series.

This list is complete through the fourteenth Series. Emma produced at least thirty Series of Bible Interpretations.

She followed the Bible Passages provided by the International Committee of Clerics who produced the Bible Quotations for each year's use in churches all over the world.

Emma used these for her column of Bible Interpretations in both the Christian Science Magazine, at her Seminary and in the Chicago Inter-Ocean Newspaper.

First Series

July 5 - September 27, 1891

Lesson 1	The Word Made Flesh *John 1:1-18*	July 5th
Lesson 2	Christ's First Disciples John 1:29-42	July 12th
Lesson 3	All Is Divine Order *John 2:1-1*1 (Christ's first Miracle)	July 19th
Lesson 4	Jesus Christ and Nicodemus *John 3:1-17*	July 26th
Lesson 5	Christ at Samaria *John 4:5-26* (Christ at Jacob's Well)	August 2nd
Lesson 6	Self-condemnation *John 5:17-30* (Christ's Authority)	August 9th
Lesson 7	Feeding the Starving *John 6:1-14* (The Five Thousand Fed)	August 16th
Lesson 8	The Bread of Life *John 6:26-40* (Christ the Bread of Life)	August 23rd
Lesson 9	The Chief Thought *John 7:31-34* (Christ at the Feast)	August 30th
Lesson 10	Continue the Work *John 8:31-47*	September 6th
Lesson 11	Inheritance of Sin *John 9:1-11, 35-38* (Christ and the Blind Man)	September 13th
Lesson 12	The Real Kingdom *John 10:1-16* (Christ the Good Shepherd)	September 20th
Lesson 13	In Retrospection	September 27th Review

Second Series

October 4 - December 27, 1891

Lesson 1	Mary and Martha *John 11:21-44*	October 4th
Lesson 2	Glory of Christ *John 12:20-36*	October 11th
Lesson 3	Good in Sacrifice *John 13:1-17*	October 18th
Lesson 4	Power of the Mind *John 14:13; 15-27*	October 25th
Lesson 5	Vines and Branches *John 15:1-16*	November 1st
Lesson 6	Your Idea of God *John 16:1-15*	November 8th
Lesson 7	Magic of His Name *John 17:1-19*	November 15th
Lesson 8	Jesus and Judas *John 18:1-13*	November 22nd
Lesson 9	Scourge of Tongues *John 19:1-16*	November 29th
Lesson 10	Simplicity of Faith *John 19:17-30*	December 6th
Lesson 11	Christ is All in All *John 20: 1-18*	December 13th
Lesson 12	Risen With Christ *John 21:1-14*	December 20th
Lesson 13	The Spirit is Able Review of Year	December 27th

Third Series

January 3 - March 27, 1892

Lesson 1	A Golden Promise *Isaiah 11:1-10*	January 3rd
Lesson 2	The Twelve Gates *Isaiah 26:1-10*	January 10th
Lesson 3	Who Are Drunkards *Isaiah 28:1-13*	January 17th
Lesson 4	Awake Thou That Sleepest *Isaiah 37:1-21*	January 24th
Lesson 5	The Healing Light *Isaiah 53:1-21*	January 31st
Lesson 6	True Ideal of God *Isaiah 55:1-13*	February 7th
Lesson 7	Heaven Around Us *Jeremiah 31 14-37*	February 14th
Lesson 8	But One Substance *Jeremiah 36:19-31*	February 21st
Lesson 9	Justice of Jehovah *Jeremiah 37:11-21*	February 28th
Lesson 10	God and Man Are One *Jeremiah 39:1-10*	March 6th
Lesson 11	Spiritual Ideas *Ezekiel 4:9, 36:25-38*	March 13th
Lesson 12	All Flesh is Grass *Isaiah 40:1-10*	March 20th
Lesson 13	The Old and New Contrasted Review	March 27th

Fourth Series

April 3 - June 26, 1892

Lesson 1	Realm of Thought *Psalm 1:1-6*	April 3rd
Lesson 2	The Power of Faith *Psalm 2:1-12*	April 10th
Lesson 3	Let the Spirit Work *Psalm 19:1-14*	April 17th
Lesson 4	Christ is Dominion *Psalm 23:1-6*	April 24th
Lesson 5	External or Mystic *Psalm 51:1-13*	May 1st
Lesson 6	Value of Early Beliefs *Psalm 72: 1-9*	May 8th
Lesson 7	Truth Makes Free *Psalm 84:1-12*	May 15th
Lesson 8	False Ideas of God *Psalm 103:1-22*	May 22nd
Lesson 9	But Men Must Work *Daniel 1:8-21*	May 29th
Lesson 10	Artificial Helps *Daniel 2:36-49*	June 5th
Lesson 11	Dwelling in Perfect Life *Daniel 3:13-25*	June 12th
Lesson 12	Which Streak Shall Rule *Daniel 6:16-28*	June 19th
Lesson 13	See Things as They Are Review of 12 Lessons	June 26th

Fifth Series

July 3 - September 18, 1892

Lesson 1	The Measure of a Master *Acts 1:1-12*	July 3rd
Lesson 2	Chief Ideas Rule People *Acts 2:1-12*	July 10th
Lesson 3	New Ideas About Healing *Acts 2:37-47*	July 17th
Lesson 4	Heaven a State of Mind *Acts 3:1-16*	July 24th
Lesson 5	About Mesmeric Powers *Acts 4:1-18*	July 31st
Lesson 6	Points in the Mosaic Law *Acts 4:19-31*	August 7th
Lesson 7	Napoleon's Ambition *Acts 5:1-11*	August 14th
Lesson 8	A River Within the Heart *Acts 5:25-41*	August 21st
Lesson 9	The Answering of Prayer Acts 7: 54-60 - Acts 8: 1-4	August 28th
Lesson 10	Words Spoken by the Mind *Acts 8:5-35*	September 4th
Lesson 11	Just What It Teaches Us *Acts 8:26-40*	September 11th
Lesson 12	The Healing Principle Review	September 18th

Sixth Series

September 25 - December 18, 1892

Lesson 1	The Science of Christ *1 Corinthians 11:23-34*	September 25th
Lesson 2	On the Healing of Saul *Acts 9:1-31*	October 2nd
Lesson 3	The Power of the Mind Explained *Acts 9:32-43*	October 9th
Lesson 4	Faith in Good to Come *Acts 10:1-20*	October 16th
Lesson 5	Emerson's Great Task *Acts 10:30-48*	October 23rd
Lesson 6	The Teaching of Freedom *Acts 11:19-30*	October 30th
Lesson 7	Seek and Ye Shall Find *Acts 12:1-17*	November 6th
Lesson 8	The Ministry of the Holy Mother *Acts 13:1-13*	November 13th
Lesson 9	The Power of Lofty Ideas *Acts 13:26-43*	November 20th
Lesson 10	Sure Recipe for Old Age *Acts 13:44-52, 14:1-7*	November 27th
Lesson 11	The Healing Principle *Acts 14:8-22*	December 4th
Lesson 12	Washington's Vision *Acts 15:12-29*	December 11th
Lesson 13	Review of the Quarter	December 18th
Partial Lesson	Shepherds and the Star	December 25th

Seventh Series

January 1 - March 31, 1893

Lesson 1	All is as Allah Wills	January 1st
	Ezra 1	
	Khaled Knew that he was of The Genii	
	The Coming of Jesus	
Lesson 2	Zerubbabel's High Ideal	January 8th
	Ezra 2:8-13	
	Fulfillments of Prophecies	
	Followers of the Light	
	Doctrine of Spinoza	
Lesson 3	Divine Rays Of Power	January 15th
	Ezra 4	
	The Twelve Lessons of Science	
Lesson 4	Visions Of Zechariah	January 22nd
	Zechariah 3	
	Subconscious Belief in Evil	
	Jewish Ideas of Deity	
	Fruits of Mistakes	
Lesson 5	Aristotle's Metaphysician	January 27th
	Missing (See Review for summary)	
Lesson 6	The Building of the Temple	February 3rd
	Missing (See Review for summary)	
Lesson 7	Pericles and his Work in building the Temple	
	Nehemiah 13	February 12th
	Supreme Goodness	
	On and Upward	
Lesson 8	Ancient Religions	February 19th
	Nehemiah 1	
	The Chinese	
	The Holy Spirit	
Lesson 9	Understanding is Strength Part 1	February 26th
	Nehemiah 13	
Lesson 10	Understanding is Strength Part 2	March 3rd
	Nehemiah 13	
Lesson 11	Way of the Spirit	March 10th
	Esther	
Lesson 12	Speaking of Right Things	March 17th
	Proverbs 23:15-23	
Lesson 13	Review	March 24th

Eighth Series

April 2 - June 25, 1893

Lesson 1	The Resurrection	April 2nd
	Matthew 28:1-10	
	One Indestructible	
	Life In Eternal Abundance	
	The Resurrection	
	Shakes Nature Herself	
	Gospel to the Poor	
Lesson 2	Universal Energy	April 9th
	Book of Job, Part 1	
Lesson 3	Strength From Confidence	April 16th
	Book of Job, Part II	
Lesson 4	The New Doctrine Brought Out	April 23rd
	Book of Job, Part III	
Lesson 5	The Golden Text	April 30th
	Proverbs 1:20-23	
	Personification Of Wisdom	
	Wisdom Never Hurts	
	The "Two" Theory	
	All is Spirit	
Lesson 6	The Law of Understanding	May 7th
	Proverbs 3	
	Shadows of Ideas	
	The Sixth Proposition	
	What Wisdom Promises	
	Clutch On Material Things	
	The Tree of Life	
	Prolonging Illuminated Moments	
Lesson 7	Self-Esteem	May 14th
	Proverbs 12:1-15	
	Solomon on Self-Esteem	
	The Magnetism of Passing Events	
	Nothing Established by Wickedness	
	Strength of a Vitalized Mind	
	Concerning the "Perverse Heart"	

Lesson 8	Physical vs. Spiritual Power	May 21st
	Proverbs 23:29-35	
	Law of Life to Elevate the Good and Banish the Bad	
	Lesson Against Intemperance	
	Good Must Increase	
	To Know Goodness Is Life	
	The Angel of God's Presence	
Lesson 9	Lesson missing	May 28th
	(See Review for concept)	
Lesson 10	Recognizing Our Spiritual Nature	June 4th
	Proverbs 31:10-31	
	Was Called Emanuel	
	The covenant of Peace	
	The Ways of the Divine	
	Union With the Divine	
	Miracles Will Be Wrought	
Lesson 11	Intuition	June 11th
	Ezekiel 8:2-3	
	Ezekiel 9:3-6, 11	
	Interpretation of the Prophet	
	Ezekiel's Vision	
	Dreams and Their Cause	
	Israel and Judah	
	Intuition the Head	
	Our Limited Perspective	
Lesson 12	The Book of Malachi	June 18th
	Malachi	
	The Power of Faith	
	The Exercise of thankfulness	
	Her Faith Self-Sufficient	
	Burned with the Fires of Truth	
	What is Reality	
	One Open Road	
Lesson 13	Review of the Quarter	June 25th
	Proverbs 31:10-31	

Ninth Series

July 2 - September 27, 1893

Lesson 1	Secret of all Power	July 2nd
Acts 16: 6-15	The Ancient Chinese Doctrine of Taoism	
	Manifesting of God Powers	
	Paul, Timothy, and Silas	
	Is Fulfilling as Prophecy	
	The Inner Prompting.	
	Good Taoist Never Depressed	
Lesson 2	The Flame of Spiritual Verity	July 9th
Acts 16:18	Cause of Contention	
	Delusive Doctrines	
	Paul's History	
	Keynotes	
	Doctrine Not New	
Lesson 3	Healing Energy Gifts	July 16th
Acts 18:19-21	How Paul Healed	
	To Work Miracles	
	Paul Worked in Fear	
	Shakespeare's Idea of Loss	
	Endurance the Sign of Power	
Lesson 4	Be Still My Soul	July 23rd
Acts 17:16-24	Seeing Is Believing	
	Paul Stood Alone	
	Lessons for the Athenians	
	All Under His Power	
	Freedom of Spirit	
Lesson 5	(Missing) Acts 18:1-11	July 30th
Lesson 6	Missing No Lesson *	August 6th
Lesson 7	The Comforter is the Holy Ghost	August 13th
Acts 20	Requisite for an Orator	
	What is a Myth	
	Two Important Points	
	Truth of the Gospel	
	Kingdom of the Spirit	
	Do Not Believe in Weakness	

Lesson 8 *Acts 21*	Conscious of a Lofty Purpose As a Son of God Wherein Paul failed Must Give Up the Idea Associated with Publicans Rights of the Spirit	August 20th
Lesson 9 *Acts 24:19-32*	Measure of Understanding Lesser of Two Evils A Conciliating Spirit A Dream of Uplifting The Highest Endeavor Paul at Caesarea Preparatory Symbols Evidence of Christianity	August 27th
Lesson 10 *Acts 23:25-26*	The Angels of Paul Paul's Source of Inspiration Should Not Be Miserable Better to Prevent than Cure Mysteries of Providence	September 3rd
Lesson 11 *Acts 28:20-31*	The Hope of Israel Immunity for Disciples Hiding Inferiorities Pure Principle	September 10th
Lesson 12 *Romans 14*	Joy in the Holy Ghost Temperance The Ideal Doctrine Tells a Different Story Hospitals as Evidence Should Trust in the Savior	September 17th
Lesson 13 *Acts 26-19-32*	Review The Leveling Doctrine Boldness of Command Secret of Inheritance Power in a Name	September 24th

Tenth Series

October 1 – December 24, 1893

Lesson 1	*Romans 1:1-19*	October 1st
	When the Truth is Known	
	Faith in God	
	The Faithful Man is Strong	
	Glory of the Pure Motive	
Lesson 2	*Romans 3:19-26*	October 8th
	Free Grace.	
	On the Gloomy Side	
	Daniel and Elisha	
	Power from Obedience	
	Fidelity to His Name	
	He Is God	
Lesson 3	*Romans 5*	October 15th
	The Healing Principle	
	Knows No Defeat.	
	In Glorified Realms	
	He Will Come	
Lesson 4	*Romans 12:1*	October 22nd
	Would Become Free	
	Man's Co-operation	
	Be Not Overcome	
	Sacrifice No Burden	
	Knows the Future	
Lesson 5	*I Corinthians 8:1-13*	October 29th
	The Estate of Man	
	Nothing In Self	
	What Paul Believed	
	Doctrine of Kurozumi	
Lesson 6	*I Corinthians 12:1-26*	November 5th
	Science of The Christ Principle	
	Dead from the Beginning	
	St. Paul's Great Mission	
	What The Spark Becomes	
	Chris, All There Is of Man	
	Divinity Manifest in Man	
	Christ Principle Omnipotent	

Lesson 7	*II Corinthians 8:1-12* Which Shall It Be? The Spirit is Sufficient Working of the Holy Ghost	November 12th
Lesson 8	*Ephesians 4:20-32* A Source of Comfort What Causes Difference of Vision Nothing But Free Will	November 19th
Lesson 9	*Colossians 3:12-25* Divine in the Beginning Blessings of Contentment Free and Untrammeled Energy	November 26th
Lesson 10	*James 1* The Highest Doctrine A Mantle of Darkness The Counsel of God Blessed Beyond Speaking	December 3rd
Lesson 11	*I Peter 1* Message to the Elect Not of the World's Good	December 10th
Lesson 12	*Revelation 1:9* Self-Glorification The All-Powerful Name Message to the Seven Churches The Voice of the Spirit	December 17th
Lesson 13	Golden Text Responding Principle Lives Principle Not Hidebound They Were Not Free Minded	December 24th
Lesson 14	Review It is Never Too Late The Just Live by Faith An Eternal Offer Freedom of Christian Science	December 31st

Eleventh Series

January 1 – March 25, 1894

Lesson 1	*Genesis 1:26-31 & 2:1-3*	January 7th
	The First Adam	
	Man: The Image of Language Paul and Elymas	
Lesson 2	*Genesis 3:1-15*	January 14th
	Adam's Sin and God's Grace	
	The Fable of the Garden	
	Looked-for Sympathy	
	The True Doctrine	
Lesson 3	*Genesis 4:3-13*	January 21st
	Types of the Race	
	God in the Murderer	
	God Nature Unalterable	
Lesson 4	*Genesis 9:8-17*	January 28th
	God's Covenant With Noah	
	Value of Instantaneous Action	
	The Lesson of the Rainbow	
Lesson 5	I Corinthians 8:1-13	February 4th
	Genesis 12:1-9	
	Beginning of the Hebrew Nation	
	No Use For Other Themes	
	Influence of Noble Themes	
	Danger In Looking Back	
Lesson 6	*Genesis 17:1-9*	February 11th
	God's Covenant With Abram	
	As Little Children	
	God and Mammon	
	Being Honest With Self	
Lesson 7	*Genesis 18:22-23*	February 18th
	God's Judgment of Sodom	
	No Right Nor Wrong In Truth	
	Misery Shall Cease	
Lesson 8	*Genesis 22:1-13*	February 25th
	Trial of Abraham's Faith	
	Light Comes With Preaching	
	You Can Be Happy NOW	

Lesson 9	*Genesis 25:27-34*	March 4th
	Selling the Birthright	
	"Ye shall be Filled"	
	The Delusion Destroyed	
Lesson 10	*Genesis 28:10-22*	March 11th
	Jacob at Bethel	
	Many Who Act Like Jacob	
	How to Seek Inspiration	
	Christ, the True Pulpit Orator	
	The Priceless Knowledge of God	
Lesson 11	*Proverbs 20:1-7*	March 18th
	Temperance	
	Only One Lord	
	What King Alcohol Does	
	Stupefying Ideas	
Lesson 12	*Mark 16:1-8*	March 25th
	Review and Easter	
	Words of Spirit and Life	
	Facing the Supreme	
	Erasure of the Law	
	Need No Other Friend	

Twelfth Series

April 1 – June 24, 1894

Lesson 1	*Genesis 24:30, 32:09-12*	April 8th
	Jacob's Prevailing Prayer	
	God Transcends Idea	
	All To Become Spiritual	
	Ideas Opposed to Each Other	April 1st
Lesson 2	*Genesis 37:1-11*	
	Discord in Jacob's Family	
	Setting Aside Limitations	
	On the Side of Truth	
Lesson 3	*Genesis 37:23-36*	April 15th
	Joseph Sold into Egypt	
	Influence on the Mind	
	Of Spiritual Origin	
Lesson 4	*Genesis 41:38-48*	April 22nd
	Object Lesson Presented in	
	the Book of Genesis	
Lesson 5	*Genesis 45:1-15*	April 29th
	"With Thee is Fullness of Joy"	
	India Favors Philosophic Thought	
	What These Figures Impart	
	The Errors of Governments	
Lesson 6	*Genesis 50:14-26*	May 6th
	Changes of Heart	
	The Number Fourteen	
	Divine Magicians	
Lesson 7	*Exodus 1:1-14*	May 13th
	Principle of Opposites	
	Power of Sentiment	
	Opposition Must Enlarge	
Lesson 8	*Exodus 2:1-10*	May 20th
	How New Fires Are Enkindled	
	Truth Is Restless	
	Man Started from God	
Lesson 9	*Exodus 3:10-20*	May 27th
	What Science Proves	
	What Today's Lesson Teaches	
	The Safety of Moses	

Lesson 10	*Exodus 12:1-14*	June 3rd
	The Exodus a Valuable Force	
	What the Unblemished Lamp Typifies	
	Sacrifice Always Costly	
Lesson 11	*Exodus 14:19-29*	June 10th
	Aristides and Luther Contrasted	
	The Error of the Egyptians	
	The Christian Life not Easy	
	The True Light Explained	
Lesson 12	*Proverbs 23:29-35*	June 17th
	Heaven and Christ will Help	
	The Woes of the Drunkard	
	The Fight Still Continues	
	The Society of Friends	
Lesson 13	*Proverbs 23:29-35*	June 24th
	Review	
	Where is Man's Dominion	
	Wrestling of Jacob	
	When the Man is Seen	

Thirteenth Series

	July 1 – September 30, 1894	
Lesson 1	The Birth of Jesus	July 1st
	Luke 2:1-16	
	No Room for Jesus	
	Man's Mystic Center	
	They glorify their Performances	
Lesson 2	Presentation in the Temple	July 8th
	Luke 2:25-38	
	A Light for Every Man	
	All Things Are Revealed	
	The Coming Power	
	Like the Noonday Sun	
Lesson 3	Visit of the Wise Men	July 15th
	Matthew 1:2-12	
	The Law Our Teacher	
	Take neither Scrip nor Purse	
	The Star in the East	
	The Influence of Truth	
Lesson 4	Flight Into Egypt	July 22nd
	Mathew 2:13-23	
	The Magic Word of Wage Earning	
	How Knowledge Affect the Times	
	The Awakening of the Common People	
Lesson 5	The Youth of Jesus	July 29th
	Luke 2:40-52	
	Your Righteousness is as filthy Rags	
	Whatsoever Ye Search, that will Ye Find	
	The starting Point of All Men	
	Equal Division, the Lesson Taught by Jesus	
	The True Heart Never Falters	
Lesson 6	The "All is God" Doctrine	August 5th
	Luke 2:40-52	
	Three Designated Stages of Spiritual Science	
	Christ Alone Gives Freedom	
	The Great Leaders of Strikes	
Lesson 7	Missing	August 12th
Lesson 8	First Disciples of Jesus	August 19th
	John 1:36-49	
	The Meaning of Repentance	

	Erase the Instructed Mind	
	The Necessity of Rest	
	The Self-Center No Haltered Joseph	
Lesson 9	The First Miracle of Jesus	August 26th
	John 2:1-11	
	"I Myself am Heaven or Hell"	
	The Satan Jesus Recognized	
	The Rest of the People of God	
	John the Beholder of Jesus	
	The Wind of the Spirit	
Lesson 10	Jesus Cleansing the Temple	September 2nd
	John 2:13-25	
	The Secret of Fearlessness	
	Jerusalem the Symbol of Indestructible Principle	
	What is Required of the Teacher	
	The Whip of Soft Cords	
Lesson 11	Jesus and Nicodemus	September 9th
	John 3:1-16	
	Metaphysical Teaching of Jesus	
	Birth-Given Right of Equality	
	Work of the Heavenly Teacher	
Lesson 12	Jesus at Jacob's Well	September 16th
	John 4:9-26	
	The Question of the Ages	
	The Great Teacher and Healer	
	"Because I Live, Ye shall Live Also."	
	The Faith That is Needful	
Lesson 13	Daniel's Abstinence	September 23rd
	Daniel 1:8-20	
	Knowledge is Not All	
	Between the Oriental and Occidental Minds	
	The Four Servants of God	
	The Saving Power of Good	
	The Meeting-Ground of Spirit and Truth	
Lesson 14	Take With You Words	September 30th
	John 2:13-25	
Review	Healing Comes from Within	
	The Marthas and Marys of Christianity	
	The Summing up of The Golden Texts	

Fourteenth Series

October 7 – December 30, 1894

Lesson 1	Jesus At Nazareth	October 7th
Luke 4:16-30	Jesus Teaches Uprightness	
	The Pompous Claim of a Teacher	
	The Supreme One No Respecter of Persons	
	The Great Awakening	
	The Glory of God Will Come Back	
Lesson 2	The Draught of Fishes	October 14th
Luke 5:1-11	The Protestant Within Every Man	
	The Cry of Those Who Suffer	
	Where the Living Christ is Found	
Lesson 3	The Sabbath in Capernaum	October 21st
Mark 1:21-34	Why Martyrdom Has Been a Possibility	
	The Truth Inculcated in Today's Lesson	
	The Injustice of Vicarious Suffering	
	The Promise of Good Held in the Future	
Lesson 4	The Paralytic Healed	October 28th
Mark 2:1-12	System Of Religions and Philosophy	
	The Principle Of Equalization	
	The Little Rift In School Methods	
	What Self-Knowledge Will Bring	
	The Meaning Of The Story of Capernaum	
Lesson 5	Reading of Sacred Books	November 4th
Mark 2:23-38	The Interior Qualities	
Mark 2:1-4	The Indwelling God	
	Weakness Of The Flesh	
	The Unfound Spring	
Lesson 6	Spiritual Executiveness	November 11th
Mark 3:6-19	The Teaching Of The Soul	
	The Executive Powers Of The Mind	
	Vanity Of Discrimination	
	Truth Cannot Be Bought Off	
	And Christ Was Still	
	The Same Effects For Right And Wrong	
	The Unrecognized Splendor Of The Soul	

Lesson 7	Twelve Powers Of The Soul	November 18th

Luke 6:20-31 The Divine Ego in Every One
Spiritual Better than Material Wealth
The Fallacy Of Rebuke
Andrew, The Unchanging One

Lesson 8 Things Not Understood Attributed to Satan
Mark 3:22-35 True Meaning Of Hatha Yoga   November 25th
The Superhuman Power Within Man
The Problem of Living and Prospering
Suffering Not Ordained for Good
The Lamb in the Midst shall Lead

Lesson 9 Independence of Mind   December 2nd
Luke 7:24-35 He that Knoweth Himself Is Enlightened
The Universal Passion for Saving Souls
Strength From knowledge of Self
Effect Of Mentally Directed Blows

Lesson 10 The Gift of Untaught wisdom   December 9th
Luke 8:4-15 The Secret Of Good Comradeship
The Knower That Stands in Everyone
Laying Down the Symbols
Intellect The Devil Which Misleads
Interpretation Of The Day's Lesson

Lesson 11 The Divine Eye Within   December 16th
Matthew 5:5-16 Knowledge Which Prevails Over Civilization
The Message Heard By Matthew
The Note Which shatters Walls Of Flesh

Lesson 12 Unto Us a Child I s Born   December 23rd
Luke 7:24-35 The Light That is Within
Significance Of The Vision of Isaiah
Signs of the Times
The New Born Story Of God
Immaculate Vision Impossible To None

Lesson 13 Review   December 30th
Isaiah 9:2-7 That Which Will Be Found In The Kingdom
Situation Of Time And Religion Reviewed
Plea That Judgment May Be Righteous
The Souls Of All One And Changeless

Made in the USA
Charleston, SC
23 September 2012